Dan Gets a Minivan

Life at the Intersection of Dude and Dad

Dan Zevin

SCRIBNER

New York   London   Toronto   Sydney   New Delhi

Scribner
A Division of Simon & Schuster, Inc.
1230 Avenue of the Americas
New York, NY 10020

First Scribner trade paperback edition May 2013

SCRIBNER and design are registered trademarks of The Gale Group, Inc.,
used under license by Simon & Schuster, Inc., the publisher of this work.

For information about special discounts for bulk purchases,
please contact Simon & Schuster Special Sales at 1-866-506-1949
or business@simonandschuster.com.

The Simon & Schuster Speakers Bureau can bring authors to your live event.
For more information or to book an event contact the Simon & Schuster Speakers
Bureau at 1-866-248-3049 or visit our website at www.simonspeakers.com.

Minivan illustration courtesy of iStock.com

Manufactured in the United States of America

2   3   4   5   6   7   8   9   10

Library of Congress Control Number: 2011040906

ISBN 978-1-4516-0646-1
ISBN 978-1-4516-0647-8 (pbk)
ISBN 978-1-4516-5614-5 (ebook)

A different version of "A New Jersey Pilgrim's Progress"
previously appeared in *Boston* magazine.

To my mother.
Thanks for all the Tuesdays.

Slow ride, take it easy
Slow ride, take it easy
(Repeat)
—Foghat

Contents

Dan Gets a Minivan

My Cup Holders Runneth Over

Most men drift through life in a fog, waiting for some moment of clarity to give them purpose and meaning. I should know; I used to be one of them. But then something changed. On an ordinary afternoon not long ago, I drove home from the dealership in my tricked-out new minivan.

"Daddy, it's awesome!" Leo shouted, bursting out the front door with his little sister, equally ecstatic. He was just five at the time, and Josie was two. It didn't take much to blow their little minds—a new Bionicle for him, a red M&M for her—but I'd never seen them quite so overcome as the first time they witnessed that magical miniature van. My wife, Megan, came rushing out after them, nearly getting toppled by our dog, Chloe, who jumped up on her hind legs and drooled on the driver's side door. The next thing I knew, we were on our first family joyride. And when I say joy, I'm talking *joy*. From that moment on, I accepted my destiny; came to terms with my fate. For I am the man in the minivan. And now, I rejoice. I rejoice every day for my collapsible third row of seats, my built-in DVD player, the bounty of cup holders I am blessed to behold.

Long ago, you see, my life was economy-size. There was room for just three passengers: Me, Me, and Me. Where we were headed was anyone's guess, for in my younger years, I was lost; blind to the miracle of a Bluetooth-compatible GPS system equipped with advanced split-screen controls. I had a radar detector instead.

How it all changed is a bit of a blur. There was a wedding, and then there was a puppy. A home was purchased in New England. A wife was promoted and transferred to New York. A town house in Brooklyn. A new baby boy. A new baby girl. A stay-at-home dad was born. A prescription for Xanax was filled. Gray hairs grew in, gray hairs fell out. Six years passed in six seconds. And then came the minivan.

So don't give me any aggravation, alright? I've heard it all a million times. "Does the driver's manual teach you how to be boring?" joked my hipster friend, Max, who lives in the town house next door with his groovy wife and cutting-edge five-year-old, though they may as well be living in some alternate universe inhabited by impossibly cool Brooklyn families who have no use for any vehicle that's not yellow with a meter on the dashboard. My younger brother, Richie, gave me a bumper sticker that said "My other car is an aircraft carrier." And some random schmuck on a Vespa—a kid who wasn't even wearing a helmet—felt entitled to remark as follows: "Betcha get a lotta ass with that car."

I was at a red light, on my way to feed the ducks in Prospect Park. "That's right, buddy," I answered. "Your mother rode shotgun last night." He flipped me off, but my kids didn't see. They were in the backseats (plural) glued to Toy Story 3. Have I already told you my minivan has a built-in DVD player? If I did, I feel it's worth repeating. My wife only lets them watch it on long trips, but what she doesn't know won't hurt her. When she's off at work all day, a "long trip" refers to anything longer than sixty seconds.

I used to be more like her. I worried about too much TV, too many gummy worms, too many toys and not enough books. But then I stopped fighting it. I gave in to it all. And now it is I you'll find at the wheel, riding high in my captain's chair. That's what we call them in the minivan scene. Captain's chairs. Remember bucket seats? They're like those, only bigger and more spectacular. If you are considering getting a minivan—and if you're not, I feel sorry for you—I'd recommend the captain's chairs without hesitation. With each passenger happily confined to his or her personal sitting arena, hair will not be pulled, wet fingers will not be inserted into neighboring ears, thoughts of corporeal punishment will not be taken under serious consideration. No. When you enter my vehicle, the first thing you'll observe is how orderly it is. Also cleanly. When a man takes pride in his achievement, he has a standing appointment at Park Slope Suds 'N' Simonizing every Friday morning at 9:30 sharp. Here is just a partial inventory of debris you will never find in my minivan (after this Friday morning at 9:30 sharp):

> ➤ banana peel and parts
> ➤ chunk of soy dog
> ➤ fur of real dog
> ➤ school of Pepperidge Farm goldfish
> ➤ string cheese (aged)
> ➤ unknown

It was November of 2007 when I first started fantasizing about minivans. Josie had recently been born, bringing the grand total of our family to five: two adults, two children, and one obese Labrador mutt who preferred being driven rather than walked. We took a lot of road trips that year. Let me rephrase that. We took a lot of sedan trips. Megan and I had the same two-door jalopy we'd been driving since we were footloose and child-free. In those days, we'd toss our backpacks in the trunk and get to wherever at whatever o'clock. But by November of 2007, something felt different. Specifically: the trunk.

We decided to drive down to Maryland so Leo and Josie could spend Thanksgiving with their cousins. According to MapQuest, it was supposed to take four hours. I spent the first five packing the trunk. At least that's what it felt like until it became clear that the portacrib needed to be strapped to the roof, and the co-sleeper, Jolly Jumper, and top half of the bathtub seat would be traveling as passengers rather than cargo. Leo covered the Jersey Turnpike in tears, but at least his shrieks were muffled by Chloe's tail, which was in front (and inside) of his mouth. He calmed down once Megan climbed into the back with an Etch A Sketch, wedging herself into a sliver of space between the two car seats. Josie woke up in Delaware when a tote bag of pop-up books crashed down on her head. That was my fault. I stopped short due to poor visibility. It was hard to see with the Baby Einstein crib mobile dangling over the mirror.

So this is how we got around for the next couple of years, until things went from bad to worse. On a five-hour sedan trip to see our old neighbors in Somerville, Massachusetts, it became painfully clear that Josie had developed a dependency on "Toot, Toot, Chugga Chugga, Big Red Car," by the Wiggles. Not "Mitten the Kitten," not "Farewell to the Wiggly Trail," just "Toot, Toot, Chugga Chugga, Big Red Car." We had to play it a million hundred times in a row or else she would wail. As you might imagine, there is a wide variety of audio selections I'd rather hear on a five-hour sedan trip than "Toot, Toot,

Chugga, Chugga, Big Red Car." One that comes to mind is a five-hour test of the emergency broadcasting system. Thanks to my minivan, that issue is moot. My dealer threw in a couple of wireless headsets to go with the kids' DVD player (built-in). Now they can listen, and I can get back to the 24-hour Pearl Jam station on satellite radio. Yes, it also came with that.

Such is the promise my minivan holds. Children are seen and not heard. Parents complete full sentences without interruption. Friends and family share special times in the collapsible third row of seats. Seriously, it's like a living room back there, only better because everyone gets their own air vent and cup holder. Why don't you stop by some time so I can show you around? I can't wait to see your reaction when I reveal the secret fold-out compartment under Leo's seat. It happens to safeguard the finest pretzel rods money can buy. They're from Costco, just one of the far-flung destinations my minivan has led me to lately. She's taken me places I never dreamed I would go, from the Brooklyn Children's Museum to the Staten Island Children's Museum to the Children's Museum of Manhattan. Why, just last weekend, she took me and my wife out to the burbs.

We had an appointment with a Realtor to look at a house. It was your basic split-level colonial, the kind of thing you just can't find in the city, not even here in Brooklyn—big yard, two-car garage, and a neighborhood playground notable not only for what it had (grass) but also for what it didn't (a sign at the entrance that warned: Rat Poison in This Area). It would be tough to leave our little brick town house in Brooklyn, but, year after year, it's been shrinking—just like that old sedan. And year after year, our friends have been moving—to the Westchesters, Montclairs, and Winnetkas of the world. The schools are better, they tell us, and you get more house for the money. I would have called them quitters a while ago, but I don't rule anything out anymore. When a man gets a minivan, he becomes open-minded; his priorities change.

So come along, won't you? Come through my sliding rear doors and pull up a captain's chair. We don't even have to go anyplace. We can just sit here with the emergency brake on, like I do by myself some nights when I need to unwind. A guy can go kind of crazy spending all day with his kids, you know what I'm saying? How about we split a fat pretzel rod and just chill for a while? You want to see a movie? I've got *Pirates of the Caribbean* in the glove compartment. We won't even have to fast-forward past the scary part. Or we can skip the movie and just crack open a few juice boxes.

Come on in, live a little, what's your rush? The way I look at it, we're in this thing together. When life deals you a minivan, you might as well enjoy the ride.

Every Dog Has His Day (in Court)

The squad car pulled up just as I was about to remove my cell phone from a pile of dog crap. It was a crisp winter morning in Fort Greene Park, and I was out for my daily constitutional with the kids—our birth daughter, Josephine, and our first child, Chloe, whom we adopted from the ASPCA eight years earlier. Ever since my son started kindergarten, mornings were just me and the gals. And I was rather pleased with myself on this particular morning. After some earlier, harrowing attempts to push Josie in her stroller while simultaneously walking Chloe on her leash (including a brief experiment which revealed that Lab mutts make lousy sled dogs), I was proud to be wearing the Gerry TrailTech Backpack Baby Carrier I found on craigslist for eleven bucks. With Josie in the backpack instead of the stroller, everybody was happy, especially Chloe, who no longer viewed her leash as an instrument of full-body strangulation. The three of us now maneuvered nimbly through the park, even when Chloe chose to conduct her business off-trail. Which is what she did seconds before the squad car pulled up.

I was in the midst of a deep knee bend, plastic bag already in hand, when Chloe surprised me by tearing off after a squirrel. I lost my grip, lost my balance, and landed on all fours myself, hovering directly over her steaming deposit. Josie found the whole thing amusing, but she wasn't the one whose cell phone flew out of her shirt pocket in the process. I watched helplessly as it sank into doody like a rock into quicksand. The only part left peeking through the poop was the tiny window showing that it was now 9:05 a.m.

"Posted at the entrance of the park is a large sign stating that dogs are not allowed off-leash after nine a.m.," the officer sneered through her car window. "So tell me, is it that you can't read or you can't tell time?"

This isn't the way a guy generally wants to be talked to with his daughter in front of him. But, to give the officer the benefit of the doubt, Josie wasn't actually in front of me. She was in back of me. And one thing I'd been noticing lately about my Gerry TrailTech Backpack Baby Carrier was that people sometimes didn't see her back there at first. As soon as they did, though, they could hardly help themselves. "Kitchee-kitchee-koo," they would remark, or "Gimme some sugar, sweet thing." One time I was crossing a busy intersection with her strapped to my shoulders when some 600-pound tow-truck driver leaned on his horn and started honking at us. I chalked it up to road rage until he craned his neck out the window and yelled, "Yo! Little lady's got the best seat in da house!"

I turned around so the law enforcement officer could see cute little Josie sitting in her backpack.

"I sure do hope Daddy got some identification," she informed her.

We weren't getting off on the right foot.

"Come on, my dog was off-leash for like two seconds," I said. "She broke away when I bent down to clean up her—"

"ID."

"Look, I'd really appreciate if you could cut me some sla—"

"ID."

"But she's not even off-leash, technically speaking. Look at her." Chloe was gallivanting back toward us, tongue waving to and fro, leash trailing behind from her collar. I grabbed it off the ground in the nick of time. One more inch and it would have suffered the same fate as my phone.

"ID."

"I don't have ID, alright? I never carry my wallet when I come to this park."

Between you and me, I did have ID and I always carry my wallet when I go to that park. I figured she'd give me a warning and drive off to engage in police harassment someplace else.

"No ID?" she said. "Then I guess I'll have to take you to the station and ID you there." She got out of the car and opened the back door like we were all supposed to hop inside—me, Josie, and Chloe, off to the station for our mug shots. Was this a practical joke? Was I getting punk'd? Or was evil incarnate really driving the beat at Fort Greene Park?

"Daddy, Daddy! Josie wanna take a ride in da police car!"

Evil incarnate was really driving the beat at Fort Greene Park.

"But *why* can't Josie take a ride in da police car, Daddy?!"

I told her it was because there was no car seat inside. It occurred to me that it must be illegal to drive a toddler around without a car seat, but it didn't seem like a great time to bring that up with the officer.

"Officer, I'm sorry, okay? How about if you fine me for having her off-leash and I'll pay it right here." As a show of good faith, I even reached for my wallet.

"Oh, so you were *lying* about not having your wallet."

I looked her straight in the eyes. They were opaque yellow, as I recall. I also observed small, blunt horns protruding from her head.

"Would you mind not calling me a liar in front of my daughter?"

"ID," she answered.

I relinquished my ID. And as she sat in her car composing what promised to be the most comprehensive ticket in the annals of criminal history, there was plenty of time to address Josie's rapid-fire inquiries into our predicament. Lately, I'd been learning to spin-control my responses to protect her from the truth. If nothing else, this was a perfect chance to practice.

"What we waiting for, Daddy?"

"Well, we're waiting for the pretty police officer here to give us a very special piece of orange paper called a ticket, princess." (*"Well, we're getting busted by Officer Butchy here, who just called your father a liar, princess."*)

"Why she gives us a special orange paper, Daddy?"

"Because she wants to make sure we always walk Chloe on her leash, princess." (*"Because she hates me, princess. She hates all men."*)

"Daddy, why she doesn't give us a special orange paper *now*?"

"Because she doesn't want to rush, princess. She wants to have enough time to do a good job." (*"Because she doesn't want to rush, princess. She wants to make sure the guy stealing that bike over there has enough time to do a good job, and that the crack whore by the Porta-Jon has a chance to get paid. Remember, the important thing is that Chloe never chases a squirrel again."*)

The officer at last presented the very special paper, which wasn't orange as I'd promised Josie, thus proving that Daddy was, indeed, a liar. It wasn't even a ticket. It was a summons. Nowhere on this summons did it say how much I owed. All it said was that I had to appear in court by March 31, or else I could get arrested. *Arrested.* Because my dog was off-leash in the park.

"I know you're gonna put that animal's waste products in the trash receptacle before I leave," said the officer before starting up her patrol car. She actually said "waste products" and "receptacle." And she actually sat there watching as I squatted down, Josie still on my back, Chloe reined in on a death-grip leash. I reflected upon my cell phone for a moment. Could I put it in the dishwasher or would water make it worse? Maybe I could have it dry-cleaned. Impatiently, the officer revved her engine. I sheathed my hand with a protective plastic bag and chucked the entire pile, cell phone and all, into the garbage can. Receptacle.

"Have a nice day," she said.

"Thank you, Officer." (*"Fuck you, Officer."*)

The Criminal Court Building is located in a neighborhood of Manhattan that has never known the light of the sun. It could be a blindingly bright afternoon across every climactic zone in the hemisphere, and the sky in this part of town would remain the color of diesel exhaust. It might be the last stretch of New York that hasn't been given a cute, Realtor-friendly nickname. It's not SoHo or NoHo or DUMBO. Come to think of it, a good name would be ScaFo, because its one distinguishing feature is that the whole place seems to be covered in scaffolding. I guess this would explain the absence of daylight. It could also explain why everyone here is always lost, including me, even on my second attempted visit.

My first attempt had been a week earlier. I was planning to blow the whole thing off, but a friendly reminder came in the mail saying a warrant for my arrest could be issued if I missed my court date. In the interest of avoiding a life behind bars, I arrived in ScaFo at three o'clock to clear Chloe's name. I wandered under scaffolding for forty-five minutes before finding the courthouse. It was next to a Dumpster, near a bar called Kegz. Inside, I was met by a walk-through metal detector and several armed security personnel who rummaged through my messenger bag before sending it through the X-ray machine. By the time they finished searching me, it was four o'clock. Coincidentally enough, four o'clock was also closing time.

I set an ETA of 2:30 for my next attempted appearance, including an extra twenty-minute cushion for scaffold navigation. The metal detector guy seemed to remember me, which sounds more impressive than it is, since I was probably the only convict he'd seen all month wearing a corduroy cap from J. Crew (eggplant) instead of a do-rag. A do-rag, in case you're not up on your gang-inspired fashion accessories, is a black bandanna made of some kind of stretchy, panty-hosey fabric. The reason I know it's called a do-rag is because every time the metal detector guy announced that we had to remove our do-rags before going upstairs to plead our cases, off came all the panty hose hats. Never in all my days have I felt quite so Caucasian. Even the other white guy had a do-rag (in addition to a neck tattoo shaped like a scorpion). He also had an empty belt holster. It wasn't empty because he used to keep his cell phone in it before it fell into fecal matter. It was empty because the security guard guy confiscated all switchblades upon arrival.

Conversation stopped when my fellow perpetrators saw me in the corner of the elevator. I wasn't even in the clinker yet, but already I felt like fresh meat—Kosher for Passover.

As it turned out, they were a fun bunch of guys, especially Muhammad Ali (no relation). Muhammad Ali stood behind me in the line upstairs. He was wearing a wife beater, but I doubted that was his actual crime because he looked too young to be married. All in all, he was very laid-back. The last time he was here, he told me, it was for underage drinking. He sweet-talked the judge into dismissing his case and was sure his foolproof technique would work again today. I was all ears, needless to say.

"I didn't show no disrespect to the judge, know what I'm sayin'? I stood up real straight and said, 'Your Honor, I made a mistake and I promise it will never happen again. Under no circumstance. You got my word."

I asked what he was in for this time around.

"Underage drinking," he replied.

He then reiterated the part about how he stood up straight. He couldn't stress enough the importance of standing up straight. To hear Muhammad Ali tell it, you'd think a person's entire defense rested upon his posture. Looking me up and down, he seemed concerned. And with good reason, too. Far be it from me to cast aspersions upon the Gerry TrailTech Backpack Baby Carrier I bought on craigslist for eleven bucks, but even I had to admit that it wasn't the greatest thing that ever happened to my spinal column.

Or, as Muhammad Ali more succinctly put it: "What's wrong with you, G? You can't go in there lookin' like no Hunchback of Motordame."

I eventually made it to the front of the line and walked over to a clerk seated behind bulletproof glass. Judging from her pallor, she had not journeyed to the other side of the glass for many, many years. As I stood there wondering whether I'd ever been so aggressively ignored by another member of the human race, I glanced back at Muhammad Ali. He thrust his chest out and saluted me like a soldier, his way of urging me to stand up straight. I did, and sure enough, the clerk suddenly looked up and noted my existence. She then looked down and noted her fingernail. She then produced a scissor from her purse and trimmed her fingernail. She then proceeded to freak me out by completely removing her fingernail from her finger. I slid my summons through the slat at the bottom of her glass, where it remained, next to her nail. In a surprise move, she took it. She then produced a bottle of nail polish.

"The judge is done with advanced cases today," she said, painting her amputated nail right there on the desk like it was an art project. I asked what she meant by "advanced cases," and she explained that the date stamped on my summons was still a week away. I'm using "explained" in the most generous possible sense of the word, by the way. When I noted that the summons itself said I had to be here by *or before* the date stamped, she further explained:

"Do you need me to repeat myself?"

I looked away as she used some kind of special finger glue to reattach her freshly manicured, severed nail.

"Yeah, I need you to repeat yourself. I've been waiting here over an hour already."

"The-judge-is-done-with-advanced-cases-toooo-day," she said. She exaggerated the movement of her mouth like she was talking to a lip-reader. "You, gotta, come, baaack a-noth-er time."

As far as I was concerned, this *was* another time, seeing as the last time was closing time. And this time, I wasn't leaving until I knew what time I needed to be here next time. So I asked her, for what I prayed would be the final time, what time would be the best time for a person to actually arrive here on time.

"Any time before lunchtime," she explained.

She seemed to be implying that there was some sort of standardized, universal lunchtime. If there was, nobody ever told me about it. Nevertheless, I had a feeling that if I stuck around trying to get some specifics out of this individual, the charges leveled against me would escalate from "off-leash dog" to "voluntary manslaughter."

I cut my losses and left. The beer was warm at Kegz, but what do you want for a buck fifty?

Given sufficient time to mull over the meaning of "any time before lunchtime," most reasonable persons would say a safe bet is 9 a.m. This was precisely the hour I reported to New York City Criminal Court for my third and final attempt to plead my case. I was determined to be first on line. I was not the only one determined to be first on line. I was about the 201st person determined to be first on line. Despite everything, though, it was nice to be back. I was on a first-name basis by now with the security staff, and I looked forward to the camaraderie awaiting me upstairs in line.

The man standing behind me this time was chewing on a twig. I'm sure he was an okay guy, but as a conversationalist, he was no Muhammad Ali. How could he be? There was a twig in his mouth. I didn't want to stare, but I couldn't help wondering if it was really a twig. Maybe it only resembled a twig, like beef jerky, for example, or possibly turkey jerky. Discreetly, I sniffed the air. There was no odor whatsoever coming from the twig. Earlier, I'd considered the possibility of a cinnamon stick, but now, no. It was totally a twig. And judging by the enthusiasm with which he was gnawing on it, it must have been a delicious twig, bursting with refreshing twig flavor.

I for one had never seen a person chew a twig until that point. As a matter of fact, the only creature I'd ever witnessed chewing a twig like that was Chloe herself. This was way back when she was still allowed to chew twigs. It was before Dr.

Young examined her incisors and said the reason she had bleeding, inflamed gums was because I let her chew twigs. It broke my heart to teach her the command, "No twig!" After all, it fell so soon on the heels of "No ball!" For five straight years before we uprooted her from Cambridge to New York, I threw Chloe her beloved tennis ball every day (twice a day if she was a good girl) for twenty, thirty minutes at a time. But then came that bitter winter morning when she leapt up to catch a pop fly and lost her balance on a patch of ice. Her piercing yelp seemed to echo for miles. Megan and I rushed her to a veterinary surgeon and shelled out fifteen hundred bucks to fix her hip. Throughout her convalescence, we carried her in our arms like a baby. And for a long time, she was our baby—until the human ones came along.

Chloe's status has since been downgraded to "pet." Time no longer allows for long jogs in the woods, or our annual summer road trip to Nova Scotia. Now she stays home with a dog sitter during family vacations, hard to believe considering our once firm policy of leaving her for no more than three hours maximum, and never without a rubber Kong chew toy stuffed not just with peanut butter, but with kibble *and* peanut butter. These days, she's lucky if we remember to feed her at all. I did manage to take her on a hike recently, all the way to the corner deli. I went inside to get Leo and Josie some fruit leather. It wasn't until I got home five minutes later that I realized I had left Chloe tied to a tree outside the deli. Again. Sometimes, I worry what would happen now if she ever got sprayed by a skunk like she did once when we lived back in Massachusetts. Would I really find time to do another Google search entitled "stinky dog"? Is there even a chance I'd again act on the advice of several websites suggesting that a bath in feminine hygiene products was the best remedy? God only knows what the checkout girl at CVS thought when I brought five boxes of Summer's Eve to her register. I didn't care. Before we had kids, Chloe was Daddy's little girl. But if you ask me if I'd douche my dog today? I bet I'd just let her stay stinky.

I decided it was no coincidence that I was standing on line with the chewer of twigs. It was meant to be. He was placed there by some higher power to shed meaning upon my many return visits to New York City Criminal Court. I wasn't here to dispute a summons, he seemed to suggest as he chewed ever closer toward the tip of his twig. I was here to save a relationship. A relationship between a man and his dog. A relationship that had been neglected. Never once had Chloe demonstrated an ounce of rivalry toward her two-legged siblings. She'd been nothing but professional, if somewhat stoic, since the day they appeared. It wasn't her fault that she'd been cast aside like a mongrel stepchild, it was mine. Chloe deserved more; much more. And for that, I was guilty.

For aiding and abetting her off-leash spree at Fort Greene Park on the morning in question, however, I was innocent. Which is why it really pissed me off when Judge Shenkman took one look at me and went, "Guilty, right?"

It happened later that day in Room 36, a storage space that had been redecorated to resemble a courtroom, complete with floor-to-ceiling American flags, and a poster of an elderly sneezing lady accompanied by the adage "Cover your mouth and keep your germs to yourself." The important thing was, I'd finally gotten into the same room as Judge Shenkman. He seemed like a mythical Wizard of Oz figure by now; the only man in all the land with the power to dismiss my case. As long as my posture was alright.

"Actually, I'm pleading innocent, Your Honor." I tried to maintain eye contact like Muhammad Ali would, but I wound up maintaining eyebrow contact. Judge Shenkman was totally bald, but he had the thick, furry eyebrows of a judicial Groucho Marx.

"Pleading not guilty is one option; pleading guilty is another option," the judge declared. "You're aware of your options?"

"Yes, I'm aware of my options."

"If you opt for guilty, for example, you pay a twenty-five dollar fine right now, I say sayonara, and you go home to your pooch, capiche?"

"What if I plead not guilty?"

Judge Shenkman peered down at me and raised an eyebrow. It was a feat of impressive strength.

"Ya plead not guilty, and your case goes to trial."

This statement implied that my case wasn't, at that very moment, in trial, which is pretty much what I thought it was in. But apparently, I was mistaken. Apparently, I'd have to come back yet again, because apparently, this was just an "appeal." An appeal in which an upstanding citizen would be pressured to provide false testimony so the New York City Department of Finance could collect a quick twenty-five bucks and Judge Shenkman could say sayonara to one more chump clogging the court system. It was an outrage, my fellow Americans. It was an affront to justice, liberty, and the tenets upon which this nation was founded. Then again, the dude had a point. I asked him if he could break a fifty.

Meanwhile, into Room 36 walks the twig chewer. He was almost done with it by now. I burned with curiosity. What did he do with the rest of it? Spit it out? Or chew it up like wood chips and actually ingest it, just like Chloe used to do? Good old Chloe. Loyal, loving Chloe. Neglected, rejected Chloe, who was probably gazing sadly through the window of our town house right now, feeling guilty for becoming a burden.

I looked over at the twig chewer and imagined Chloe's face staring back at me. And in that moment, I came back to my senses.

"Not guilty, Your Honor," I stated. I really wish you could have seen my posture.

My trial date was set for April 27. It would proceed not in the now-familiar ScaFo district of Manhattan, but back in my home borough of Brooklyn, where I was first accused of wrongdoing. According to the Official Notification Adjournment Slip I received on the way out, *"Si Usted no comparece, una orden de detencion podria ser emitido para Usted."* I was never exactly what you'd call an AP Spanish student, but I did appreciate the formal *usted* rather than the familiar *tú*. It was the most respect I'd received from the New York City court system so far.

Winter turned to spring, and with each passing week, I grew more anxious about my impending trial. I guess the thing I got most hung up on was whether to tell the next judge about my phone falling in the dog crap. It seemed like a detail that would help me appear sympathetic, but one that could be deemed inappropriate by a jury of my peers. After much backing-and-forthing, I decided to consult a lawyer on this one. I went straight to Maggie Roberts, Esq., an attorney with a firm called Disability Rights California. Roberts is known as one of the top lawyers specializing in health insurance rights for children with disabilities. She is also known as my sister-in-law, a qualification that more than compensated for her lack of experience in canine litigation. Maggie said to leave out the stuff about the soiled cell phone. She also said not to worry about the jury because there wouldn't be one. Other than that, her legal counsel was that she and my older brother,

Barry, were on their way out to dinner, so I should call back later if I felt like it.

The night before my arraignment, I'd written and rewritten my testimony so many times, I couldn't tell if I was coming off as sympathetic or just pathetic. Megan suggested rehearsing, so we did a little role-playing game in bed after she put the kids to sleep. Some couples play Master and Servant, we played Judge and Defendant. She was the judge. She used Leo's Little Tikes toy hammer as her gavel.

Judge Megan called court into session, and I tried out my top four opening statements to see which one Her Honor found most sympathetic.

"Because my baby girl was on my back at the time, Your Honor—"

"Not guilty!" Megan declared.

"I was cleaning up after my dog while my baby girl was on my back, Your Honor—"

"Not guilty!" Megan declared.

"In an effort to both beautify the park and be a responsible father, Your Honor—"

"Not guilty!" Megan declared.

And finally:

"So I had my innocent little baby girl on my back as I was beautifying the park by cleaning up after my dog, whom I was walking on her leash during designated on-leash hours, when suddenly and unexpectedly, a squirrel caught her attention, triggering her deep ancestral instinct to—"

"Dan, it's two o'clock in the morning, go take an Ambien," Megan declared.

I felt like a million bucks as I approached the Brooklyn Central Courts Building on the crystal clear morning of April 27.

For starters, it was an easy, ten-minute walk from our town house, eliminating the agoraphobic impulses I'd developed toward the place in ScaFo. On top of that, this place looked like a court of law was supposed to look, with the fancy Greek columns and the shiny marble floors and the leather brief-cases instead of the greasy McDonald's bags. As a matter of fact, the only thing it had in common with the ScaFo branch turned out to be the hairy-browed man in charge: none other than Judge Ira Shenkman, who clearly went wherever the work was. I found his side-splitting sense of humor oddly comforting.

"All of you are probably sitting here today wondering the same thing," he said with a straight face. "How on earth do I maintain my physique?"

Ba-dum-bum.

After the first hour, the only thing I was wondering was what I was supposed to do when (and if) it was ever my turn to take the stand. There had to be a hundred other defendants packed into the courtroom. There were those accused of disorderly conduct, of riding a bike on the sidewalk, of public urination. There were those charged with graffiti, scratchiti, possession of marijuana, "open container," hopping a subway turnstile, occupying a bus seat marked Wheelchair Priority Seating. The good news was that I was getting off easy, since I'd dabbled in a number of those crimes myself at one point or another with no arrest record to date (though someone would surely press charges for public urination if the pace didn't pick up in there soon). No matter how many defendants took the stand ahead of me, though, I remained unclear on courtroom procedure. All I could tell from the ample time I had to observe was that your name and crime would be called by the lady in the corner (the clerk?), you'd walk over to the guy with the Rasta ponytail and the three piece suit (the public defender?), and then you'd stand around like a moron while he and Judge Shenkman conversed in secret code language.

Judge: So. 00–7?
Possible Public Defender: No. DC-10.
Judge: Okay. H2O, QVC, Breaker 1–9.
Possible Public Defender: LMNOP.

Then the judge would look at the public urinator or whoever was standing there, and issue his decree. For example: "You gotta stop urinating in public, got it, kiddo?" The defendant would make a closing comment, such as "Yeah," and each case would officially conclude when the judge said the following code word: "ACD."

Even after sitting there for two hours, I still couldn't decode ACD. It seemed like ACD was good, because even the disorderly conductor glided out of the courtroom with a smile on his face after Judge Shenkman said ACD, but still, I could not be sure.

During one of several unexplained half-hour recesses, I turned to a stylish woman seated next to me and asked if perhaps she knew what the hell was going on. We'd exchanged perplexed eye-rolls throughout the proceedings, most recently when the Possible Public Defender gave the following verbatim counsel to the DVD bootlegger he was defending: "Shhhhh!" I could tell we shared similar sensibilities, me and this stylish woman seated next to me. I had a hunch that she, too, was a writer. Don't ask me why. Maybe it was the turquoise jewelry (always a giveaway), but more likely it was writer's radar. It's like gaydar, I guess. Or Jewdar, which I most certainly have. We can tell.

"Your guess is as good as mine," answered Ming Quan, *author*. I chose not to reveal our shared occupation even after confirming hers. Things tend to get weird when writers ask about each other's work, especially when they ask, "What have you been working on lately?" and the only honest answer is "my defense case." Well, that and my blog. It's not actually *my* blog, I should add while we're on the topic of defending myself. It's a nauseatingly upbeat blog I agreed to write for some guy I met at Back to School Night. He's trying to launch an online publication I'll call NewMan.com. From what I can tell from his business plan, NewMan.com is a propaganda website that tries to convince men aged thirty-five and up how awesome everything is once you're middle-aged. I prefer to think of it as OldMan.com. It's easier to come up with ideas that way. I just think of something that sucks about being a man aged thirty-five and up, then I make it sound great. The one I was working on when I encountered Ming Quan, for example, was called "Hair Loss, Your Gain!" Did I mention I used to write for paper-based publications aimed at men aged thirty-five and down? I did, until making the unfortunate career move of turning thirty-six.

All of this should explain why I elected to tell Ming Quan that I was "between gigs." "Between gigs" was something I always wanted to say. Not only did it sound cool, but also the other person would feel sorry for you and realize you didn't care to discuss it further, so the two of you could move on to more pressing issues of the day, such as what ACD means.

"I have a few theories," she said sarcastically, "but I'm leaning towards 'Apparently, Case Dismissed.'" I decided Ming was a scribe of great wit, and made a mental note to read her collected works. We went on to share a laugh over Judge Shenkman's eyebrows, but the real bonding came when Ming divulged the nature of her legal battle. It seemed she was cruising along the West Side Highway with her Yorkshire terrier when the cuddly little guy leapt into her lap. At that exact moment, a police officer drove by, noticed the dog, and pulled her over for reckless driving.

"Reckless driving?!" I said indignantly. "That's preposterous!" Well, maybe I didn't say "preposterous," but you get what I'm talking about here. I'd known her only two hours, but I'll tell you one thing about my friend Ming: she was not a person who drove recklessly. Big deal, so her dog jumped in her lap. It could've happened to anyone. In an act of unity, I offered my services as a character witness when (and if) it was ever Ming's turn to take the stand.

You can imagine the outpouring of support she demonstrated upon learning that I, too, was here on unavoidable dog-related charges. "What?! How could you possibly be expected to chase after Chloe when you were carrying your daughter, Josie, on your back? You were just trying to do the right thing!" I knew then and there that Ming was someone with whom I could entrust the most delicate details of my case. I did, and immediately afterward, she assured me there was nothing to worry about. Her cousin was a sales rep for Verizon and he could probably get me a new phone.

Our conversation was cut short when a chain gang walked in the room. I'm not someone who comes into much contact with chain gangs. Every now and then, I do see this group of preschoolers walking single file to the playground attached to a fuzzy green rope, but that's the closest thing. As for real chain gangs, like the shackled and handcuffed gentlemen who were being police-escorted into Judge Shenkman's courtroom, I have to admit it made me a little tense. Ming and I shared one of our special unspoken gestures, all turned-up palms and shaking heads. *Now we've seen everything!,* we silently agreed.

In keeping with the spirit of the day, the arrival of the chain gang went unexplained. Instead, that irrepressible Judge Shenkman tossed off another one of his trademark zingers:

"When these guys first met, they didn't even know each other. Now, they've become very attached!"

Was the chain gang a prop? A sight gag? A carefully choreographed half-time act Judge Shenkman trots out whenever he's losing his audience? Some things are not for us to know.

Somewhere between my arrival in court at 8:30 that morning and the point when it felt like the statute of limitations was about to expire on my case (and life), a guy got called to the stand for having an unlicensed dog. He was the first felon of the day not to get ACD. What exactly his sentence was, I didn't catch, because I was too busy having a private panic attack. You see, Chloe was unlicensed, too. Unleashed, no. But unlicensed? Let's just say I was suddenly guilty of a crime even more grievous than the one I was charged with. I convinced myself that it was bound to come up during my interrogation, when (and if) it was ever my turn to take the stand. How would I explain it within the confines of the truth, the whole truth, and nothing but the truth?

"If it pleases the court, Your Honor, I didn't get her a license because it just seemed like a huge pain in the ass."

"Aha!" I imagined Judge Shenkman shouting, pounding his gavel to restore order in the court. "Then it's also fair to assume that she doesn't have an up-to-date rabies vaccination!"

"With all due respect, I would contend that she's not at great risk of contracting rabies in Brooklyn."

"My good man, it is my understanding that you have taken

the stand today as a result of your dog's chronic practice of chasing squirrels."

"Objection!" the Possible Public Defender would cry. "I don't see what relevance this has upon my client's—"

"Objection overruled! Answer the question, Mr. Zevin!"

"Yeah, she chases squirrels."

"In that case, let me ask you this," Shenkman would say. "Are you by any chance aware of the single most common carrier of the rabies virus in the entire New York—New Jersey Metropolitan Area?"

"Um . . ."

"Whaddaya say I give you a hint . . ."

I envisioned Ira assuming his borscht belt persona at this point in the proceedings, wiggling his wild eyebrows up and down like a rodent.

"Anybody out there got an acorn?!" he'd yell out to the crowd, "because this guy's a nut!"

The audience would guffaw. Judge Shenkman would get his own special on Comedy Central. And I would be shackled to the chain gang and sent to the electric chair in an orange jumpsuit, mumbling "No comment" to the reporters gathered outside.

What can I tell you, the mind wanders under conditions of torture. But even if I was blowing things slightly out of proportion, there was no denying it: pleading innocent to this one little crime could lead to being found guilty of sundry bigger ones. Forget about the dog license. Did you know me in college? I could tell you some stories.

Unfortunately, it was too late to reverse my plea. And now that I'd worked myself into a state of stained armpits, it was—of course—finally my turn to testify. At least I assumed it was my turn. I mean, Don Zoovin sounds pretty much like Dan

Zevin, don't you think? My heart pounding, I walked to the podium at a pace that felt like slow motion, pausing when I reached the Possible Public Defender. He was standing at a lectern with his head buried in a book, presumably some complicated legal text outlining the ins and outs of international leash law. Glancing down, I noticed the title: *Arthur Frommer's Dollarwise Guide to the Caribbean, Including Bermuda and the Bahamas.* Was this really what he was reading, or had I slowly gone mad? I feared it was the latter. On the bright side, at least now I had a backup defense: not guilty by reason of insanity.

The Possible Public Defender looked up from his book, satisfied, I hoped, with the sightseeing opportunities recommended by Arthur Frommer, and deliberated with the judge.

Judge: So. PB&J?
Possible Public Defender: No. CDR-W.
Judge: Okay. 5–4–3–2–1.
Possible Public Defender: Fe Fi Fo Fum.

And then Judge Shenkman fixed his gaze upon me. The room was silent but for the hacking cough of a court stenographer. She was not, incidentally, covering her mouth and keeping her germs to herself.

"Mind if I ask you a question, my friend?" Judge Shenkman said. "What kind of a dog is it that you have?"

"A mutt," I replied, unsure where this line of questioning would lead.

"That's a very good kind of a dog, right?"

"Right."

"Man's best friend, am I correct?"

"Yeah, correct."

The judge then turned to the Possible Public Defender and said he had one final question. The PPD did not react. He was still standing there, but his mind had long since wandered off to the Caribbean, including Bermuda and the Bahamas. Not that it mattered anymore. F. Lee Bailey could have been defending me and it wouldn't have mattered. The judge had One Final Question. Obviously, he was about to ask what my dog's registered license number was.

Somewhere in the distance, I heard the opening bars of "Back on the Chain Gang" by the Pretenders.

"What's his name?" Shenkman said.

I didn't know what he was talking about.

"The pooch. He has a name?"

This was his One Final Question.

"*Her*," I said. "Her name is Chloe."

"Chloe."

"Yeah. Mmm-hmm."

"That's a nice name."

"Thanks."

"Chloe."

"Yup, just . . . Chloe."

"Okay," he said, without so much as a pause. "ACD."

If you find yourself at this point in my tale wondering how the honorable Judge Shenkman could arrive at his verdict without gathering any facts and/or weighing any evidence, I hate to break it to you, but you're playing a losing game. The only thing that matters is that an innocent man, aka me, was exonerated. Did the hall erupt with cries of victory as my supporters turned to each other to embrace and rejoice? Well, not exactly. I departed the courtroom to the echo of a single pair of hands, clapping. And I don't think I have to tell you that those same hands once caressed a tiny Yorkshire terrier while driving unrecklessly down the West Side Highway.

That was the last I ever saw of Ming Quan. I never even found out if she got ACD. I probably should have stuck around to get her cousin's number at Verizon, but in the end, my legal ordeal allowed me to focus on what's important. I'd promised my eldest daughter I'd be home in time to help her answer nature's call. And nobody was going to call her daddy a liar.

On No Longer Giving a Shit

I haven't given a shit in approximately five to seven years, and I'll tell you, I've never felt better. No longer do I mind that my life isn't exactly as I pictured it by the time I hit forty. Gone are the sleepless nights spent worrying when I'd make my first million; enter my first triathlon; learn how to eat a lobster right. When I die, will I have contributed anything significant to society? Ask me if I give a shit.

It's not that I've lost ambition, it's just that my ambitions have evolved, shall we say. Twenty years ago, it was my ambition to win a Pulitzer Prize. Today, it is my ambition to get a reclining chair for the living room. And not just any reclining chair. This chair needs to recline *and* swivel. The reason it needs to recline is that my lovely wife, Megan, can often be found reclining on our living room couch, where, on those cozy winter nights after she puts the kids to bed, she can curl up with six thousand pages worth of reading matter she has brought home from the office, glancing up every now and then at the crackling Duraflame in the fireplace. Far be it from me to deny her this superior living room vantage point. Yet I, too, have waited many years to live in a town house with a fireplace, and I, too, wish to recline. I also wish to face the television. Ipso facto: my ambition to swivel.

It is a lofty goal, this chair of my dreams, but once I achieve it, I will enjoy the hard-earned reward not only of reclining, but also of swiveling. Swiveling to face my fireplace, my TV, and my wife—*concurrently*. I found one in a Restoration Hardware catalog we had in the bathroom, but it had one of those clunky wooden stick shifts on the side you need to pull on to make the footrest come out. Frankly, that's a little more work than I'm willing to do after forking over fifteen hundred bucks.

There's no need to feel sorry for me, or politely reassure me that I'll recharge my career once family life settles down. Thank you for refreshing my memory about those books I once wrote, the radio spots I used to record, the column I did for that alternative weekly, which led to the one for that mainstream monthly, which led to those magazines for men thirty-five and under. With all due respect, you're missing the point when you ask if I've been blocked, unmotivated, or in some sort of slump since then. See, I made a *choice* to stop giving a shit. And now, I'm empowered by indifference. The nauseatingly upbeat content I currently provide for OldMan. com (latest post: "Forty Is the New Twenty!") is not about the Pulitzer Prize I once wished to win, it's about the Pulitzer I no longer *choose* to win. And the Joneses I no longer care to keep up with. And, by extension, in no particular order: the edgy indie band I don't feel like seeing, the trendy Vietnamese sandwich I don't plan on tasting, and the Next Big Thing I can't be bothered being. I just want the chair, you know what I'm saying? And I want it in leather, not that bullshit fake suede the lady at Pottery Barn was trying to sell me the other day.

The Effects of Procreation Upon Ambition:
A Statistical Analysis

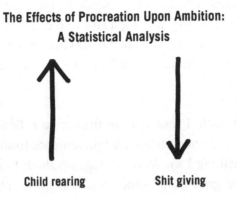

Child rearing   Shit giving

It should come as no big shocker that decreased shit giving coincides with increased child rearing. Especially since I went and sired a second one, there hasn't been time to give a shit about anything but them—particularly me. I can't tell you what a relief this has been. Back when I was a more dedicated wordsmith, I hasten to recall, I maintained a disciplined nine-to-five writing routine. Yet I was plagued by the constant doubt that I wasn't getting published enough; getting paid enough; getting anything enough. Now I am at ease. Having children gives every writer what they're *really* searching for: an excuse not to write.

Come to think of it, this is the first paragraph I've composed since last Thursday. And guess what? I've got a notion to wrap things up after the next sentence or two. There will be no beating myself up over it, no self-recrimination. Once I stopped giving a shit, I started prioritizing. For example, it's now 10:34 a.m., and I'm asking myself: If I keep sitting here, when am I going to glue the head back onto Leo's Doc Ock action figure? When will I order larvae for Josie's live-butterfly growing habitat? Each day brings a new set of yellow Post-it notes, including the one I'm just now noticing in my peripheral vision, which I stuck on my computer screen before going to sleep last night so I wouldn't forget to: *Install Josie's new car seat in minivan.* I don't know about you, but for me, that one right there is easily going to take the rest of the day. See ya.

Okay, I'm back. I took care of the car seat. Four days ago. And I haven't constructed a single sentence from then until now, something I wouldn't be bragging about before my job description grew from "writer of sentences" to "researcher of day camps, comparer of 529 college funds, and inserter of D batteries into self-propagating populations of plastic toys."

I guess this is where you might get the idea that kids can limit your success. But to you I say this: That depends on your definition of success. Myself, I now consider it a successful day if I took a shower. Which I didn't today. Or yesterday. What do you think I'm wearing this Mets cap for? You think I'm a baseball player? I'm a regular Joe. A regular, unshowered Joe who woke up this morning with some crazy Don King updo and covered it up with a baseball cap instead of taking a shower. At some point in the future, I hope to get back to showering. But for now, the whole thing feels like such a production. Between the soaping and the shampooing (not to mention the rinsing and the drying), it was sucking up twenty-two minutes every morning. That's precious time I need to prepare an English muffin for Leo, oatmeal for Josie, and yogurt with granola for Megan, who is meanwhile upstairs struggling to clothe both children in socially acceptable apparel (i.e., not underpants and snow boots, Josie's signature style). Once they finally sit down at the table, I stand over the sink and scarf down my own morning meal, which I take with cream, sugar, and a 5-Hour ENERGY chaser for that invigorating spike in blood pressure I need after a night of scary monster dreams. (Theirs, not mine—at least not usually.) Then it's off to the races with my Don King hair concealed in a baseball cap. I may not look as dapper as the Wall Street dads, but you should see me bust a move in Josie's Music for Aardvarks class.

Speaking of other dads, I would now like to tell you an interesting gender-related thing I've noticed. It is much easier for fathers than mothers to stop giving a shit in the personal appearance arena. When we dads are at the playground, we are embraced for who we are, not how we look. Strangers don't dwell upon our paunchy wine bellies, layers of fingernail schmutz, or semi-shaven faces. It doesn't matter that we started letting our nose hair grow the minute we became parents. All that matters is that we are observed in the presence of our children. Citizens are awed by our mere existence, and choose to accentuate the positive.

"How fortunate those kids are to have a strong male role model," marvel the heavily made-up mommies by the swing set. "And what smooth and silky nose hair he has, with no split ends."

These double standards of shit giving aren't skin deep, either. The ladies love a dad who has also stopped caring about his career. I'm serious. The other day when I brought Leo to a playdate at Jeremy's apartment in Brooklyn Heights, his mother went off about how great it was that I quit teaching at NYU so I could spend more time with my kids. "We need more men like you," was her exact remark. It wasn't a week earlier that I heard her slandering little Isabelle's mom for leaving her job in finance. "It's so depressing when women that successful just throw it all away and become Stepford Wives," she said.

Sometimes I feel a little bad that I no longer give a shit. But only about certain things, like, I don't know, the homeless. Well, maybe not *all* the homeless. Definitely the homeless children, though. How could someone not give a shit about the homeless children? A long time ago, I volunteered at a shelter for the homeless children. I went to the shelter every Tuesday night and read picture books to them. Sometimes I wonder what happened to that guy. That guy was a giver. A giver of shit.

And then I remind myself, "Dan, it's not that you no longer give a shit about the homeless children, it's just that now you give it in a different way—as an IRS Form 1040 charitable contribution that is tax-deductible to the full extent of the law."

This brings to light your basic bottom-line, dollars-and-cents take on not giving a shit: Money changes everything, which Cyndi Lauper so aptly put forth in her 1984 hit single, not to be confused with The Smiths' "Money Changes Everything," which was entirely instrumental, even though Bryan Ferry later added lyrics and released it as "The Right Stuff," which I only know because I used to be really into music before I stopped giving a shit about it. But anyway. If it's true that money changes everything (which it is), maybe it's equally true that the more money you get, the less shit you give.

Or maybe I've got it backwards.

The point is, you don't always see it coming. That's what happened to my friend Scott. Scott is one of the most motivated persons I know. He's a CEO or a CFO or something. Whatever he is, he has an O. And to get that O, he worked extremely hard for the past twenty-four years. When he hit the twenty-fifth, he abruptly stopped giving a shit. It happened at 6:45 p.m. last Wednesday, in the conference room.

"I was sitting there listening to my assistants describe this mentorship thing they wanted to start," he told me. "But the whole time, all I could think about was whether I was allowed to combine my miles with my wife's so we could upgrade to business class this Christmas." One thing led to another and soon they were volunteering to be on committees. Committees that would meet on weekends.

"I was like, come on, don't you people have a *life*? Then I realized, oh yeah, they're young. Work *is* their life."

The experience left Scott feeling old and jaded, so I did my best to set him straight. No, it is not possible to combine your frequent-flier miles with your wife's, I consoled him, unless you are willing to pay 135 bucks for every 10,000 miles you transfer plus additional administrative and processing fees. I know this for a fact because I tried to do it myself when I was planning our trip to Disneyland. I wound up spending like an hour on the phone trying to figure it out with some customer service representative from Continental who was either dumb or a dick, I couldn't decide, but he didn't know what he was talking about so I finally just got online and filled out the application for the Continental Visa card that gives you 20,000 bonus miles after your first purchase, which right there was enough for a free domestic roundtrip ticket. But here's the real thing I told Scott to make him feel better: You don't have to pay the annual fee if you cancel the card immediately after you get the miles.

And with that crucial tip, I would now like to end this conversation. After all, a guy could go on all day about not giving a shit. Or, he could close his laptop and take a seat in his living room, upon the magnificent purchase he made at Crate and

Barrel last week. As he concurrently swivels toward his wife, fireplace, and TV after another day of not winning the Pulitzer Prize, a guy can feel pretty certain he's not blocked, unmotivated, or in some sort of slump. He can feel pretty certain he just needs to recline.

Big Nose On Campus

As you may have figured out by now, I am not one of your can-do, role-model type of individuals who motivates future generations to carry the torch of my legacy. Oh, I guess I've impressed one or two folks along the way, but here I'm referring to those who've seen me parallel-park an automobile the size of their brownstone, or dreamed that they, too, might one day be elected to the office of Class Parent.

Recently, however, I was mistaken for someone who is inspirational. The dean of a nearby college was considering me to deliver their annual commencement address. Given the weight of this honor, I rose to the occasion with the only appropriate response: "Why?"

"What do you mean, *why*?" came the incredulous voice on the other end of the phone. "I told them you were a high-level humorist with an uncanny ability to chronicle each chapter of life."

It was Kevin MacRae, a high-level pitch man with an uncanny ability to blow smoke up my *tuchus*. Kevin is a booking agent for the college lecture circuit. It had been 150 years or so since we'd been in contact, shortly after I myself graduated from college. He cold-called me when my first high-level humor book came out. It was entitled *Entry-Level Life: A Complete Guide to Mas-*

querading as a Member of the Real World. The book was a parody of the self-help manuals my father gave me at graduation, all of which turned out to be even less useful than my diploma in securing employment that didn't require washing my hands before returning to work. Uncannily chronicling that rather humiliating chapter of life, I offered new grads firsthand tips the others lacked: How to fake a résumé; BS through a job interview; live with violently insane roommates. Kevin was convinced I'd be a campus comedy phenom not witnessed since Carrot Top.

And so it was that I launched a sideline career most aptly described in two words: (1) easy (2) money. All I had to do was show up at whatever college Kevin conned into booking me—typically one composed entirely of kids who didn't get into their backup school—and do a stand-up act lifted straight from my book. Basically, I was the warm-up band. A few weeks before the arrival of the real commencement speaker, i.e. some gray-haired geezer revealing that "life is like a book of many chapters," I'd roll into town and give them the real deal. I was not awarded a fat check or honorary degree by the dean or Board of Trustees. Instead, I flew under the radar, forever being sponsored, co-sponsored, and co-co-co-sponsored by a ragtag team of bankrupt student groups like the comedy 'zine in conjunction with the pirate radio station in association with the campus cannabis club. At one notable appearance at a community college, the name of which I can't remember, 90 percent of the crowd (nine kids) appeared to be members of the Taiwanese Student Society. Based on their vacant expressions, I speculated that they weren't fluent in English. I also figured this was how Kevin talked them into booking me.

Graduation seasons came and went, and *Entry-Level Life* slowly died—dashing Kevin's dreams of repping the next campus Carrot Top. But, to tell you the truth, the act was getting old anyway—and so was I. At a certain point, I had to ask myself: What the hell do I know about life after college anymore? I don't even know how to compose a text message. Every time I try, my new cell phone does this thing where it decides for itself what word I'm trying to type. It happened again this morning when I attempted to contact my twenty-year-old niece, Emma. Emma goes to Sarah Lawrence College, not that far from our house in Brooklyn. All I wanted to do was ask Emma to babysit this Saturday night so Megan and I could go out, to buy frameless glass shower doors. Here is what my text message looked like: *Empty, cat you babble sit Saturn?*

That's it in a nutshell, I remember thinking. Not only don't I relate to college students anymore, I can't even communicate with them.

Luckily for me, that is exactly what qualifies someone to deliver a college commencement address.

"What school?" I asked Kevin, shorthand for, "What school could possibly be desperate enough to have me be their commencement speaker?"

There was a pause on the other end of the phone, and then he said: "Are you ready?"

"For what?"

"For Cardinal MacCauley College!"

"No, not ready."

"Why not?"

"Why is it called that?"

"It's their name."

"I know it's their name. And when you pitched me to them, did you happen to mention *my* name?"

I was referring specifically to my surname: Zevin. I think it's safe to say that when you hear "Zevin," the first thing that

comes to mind probably isn't "Cardinal MacCauley College."
In fact, "Cardinal MacCauley College" probably isn't the sec-
ond or third thing that comes to mind when you hear "Zevin."
If you took a poll of every person on planet Earth, you would
find that not one of them has had the thought, "Zevin: Cardinal
MacCauley College" at any time in the history of civilization.

But Kevin MacRae is not like every person on planet Earth.
Kevin MacRae is an agent. He said he'd been booking the
commencement speaker at Cardinal MacCauley College on
and off for years, and they'd come to trust his judgment. He
said they wanted someone a little different this year; someone
who could be lighthearted; someone who could be inspirational; someone who could be at graduation this Sunday at
two o'clock.

Reflecting upon that final character trait, a couple questions came to mind. The first was: Would they pay my bus
fare, because Leo had Super Soccer Stars every Sunday at two,
so I'd have to leave the minivan at home for Megan to use. The
second was:

"Okay, who dropped out at the last minute?"

"No one!" he insisted. "They want *you*." Like all high-level
pitchmen, Kevin has an uncanny ability to talk unbelievably
fast, and for a second there, it sounded like he said, "They
want *Jew*." Which would actually explain a lot.

Still, I had a sneaking suspicion that mine was not the sort
of name that was ever on their A-list (as opposed to their
J-list). I had no idea who they *really* wanted, but, evidently,
the luck of the Irish had hit a rough patch.

"Come on, who canceled? Conan O'Brien?"

"No."

"P. J. O'Rourke?"

"No."

"Rue McClanahan?"

"Who?"

"Blanche. From *Golden Girls.*"

"Ha, a dead person! Comic gold! That's why they want *Jew* to speak in front of four thousand people."

I was sure he was lying, but I suddenly didn't care. *Four thousand people?* I thought. That's a lot of people. That's around 3,999 more people than showed up for my appearance at DeVry University in New Brunswick, New Jersey. (And 4,000 more than showed up for my gig at Framingham State.)

So maybe Kevin was right. Maybe this was my chance to step off the daddy track and get back in the game. Maybe it was time to start giving a shit again.

The next day, I awaited my phone call from the dean of Cardinal MacCauley College. The dean simply wanted to tell me about the school, according to Kevin, and say how thrilled everyone would be to host me. Translation: This was going to be a screener; a friendly little chitchat meant to judge if I was everything Kevin cracked me up to be. I was used to screeners because I got them all the time back when I was still the warm-up act. But the difference was, I never got screened by anyone with quite so terrifying a title as "Dean." The calls usually came in at 3 a.m. from some spaced-out sophomore who'd been using his phone card to cut lines of Ritalin before using it to call me. Back then, the kids doing the screeners just wanted to make sure I told lots of masturbation jokes. And you may rest assured they had nothing to worry about.

I suspected the dean of Cardinal MacCauley College had somewhat opposing motives for conducting a screener. Kevin concurred.

"I'd never ask you to reinvent yourself," he promised. "But you may want to soften your tone here and there."

The thing is, I didn't have an issue with "reinventing myself." That had magically happened on its own since those entry-level years I spent sharing my smart-aleck advice with the proud pupils of America's party schools. In gratitude, they shared their gift of free beer with me, except at this one community college where they shared their gift of free Taiwanese sake. If there is any doubt that I've "reinvented" myself since then, one only has to glance at my current social calendar: three birthday parties for Leo's friends and two for Josie's, this month alone. Also, date night with Megan every Saturday evening, which we both agree is vital to our relationship as long as we're not too tired.

With regards to "softening my tone," I figured Kevin wanted me to go through my old act and take out all the bad words. This turned out to be partially true. He wanted me to go through my old act and take out *all* the words. I was delivering a commencement speech, he reminded me. I had to be inspirational, not cynical.

"I thought I didn't have to reinvent myself," I remarked.

"You don't," Kevin replied. "I came up with a concept that's totally . . . *you*."

My sphincter tightened in fear.

"Are you ready?" he said.

"For what?" I said.

"Life is like a book of many chapters," he said.

"No, not ready."

"Why not?"

"Don't you think it's kind of cheesy? It's like a Hallmark card."

"You'll make it *funny*," Kevin said. "It's like I told the dean. You're the most influential comic talent of the postwar era."

At this point, I told Kevin to go do something to himself involving one of the bad words from my old act.

"Don't be nervous," Kevin said. "When the dean calls, just be yourself."

It sounded like pretty good advice until he told me the dean's name: Sister Kathleen.

I spotted Sister Kathleen's picture on the first page of the college alumni magazine Kevin FedExed so I could familiarize myself with the school. She was leading a ribbon-cutting ceremony in front of the newly renovated Rooney Student Center. It was a multimillion-dollar project, according to the caption, and the accompanying photos showed a state-of-the-art fitness center, computer lab, and catering hall. It was hard to focus on all these interior shots, though. I was strangely fixated on one depicting the outside of the building, and its dominant architectural feature. Here is my artist's rendering:

Above: Rooney Student Center
(artist's rendering)

I should probably note at this point that I've never been the Jewiest Jew on the block. Not that I'm the kind of Jew who collects decoy ducks or anything, but I also don't have a lot of Judaica lying around the house. I had a Bar Mitzvah. It was at B'nai Jeshrun, a temple so reformed that it was known throughout New Jersey as Our Lady of Jeshrun. When I turned thirteen, the teacher gave me a Memorex tape of some songs in another language (I'm assuming Hebrew). She said to play it in my Walkman until I could sing it by heart. On the big day, I also recall reading aloud from this cheat sheet they gave to remedial Jews. It consisted of Hebrew passages (again, I'm assuming) that were phonetically spelled out into English. All I had to do was recite the weird-sounding words without the inconvenience of knowing what I was talking about.

It was all downhill from there. One day I ate a ham sandwich, the next I married a shiksa.

But through it all, I remain a tribesman. When I hunger, do I not nosh? When I am hot, do I not schvitz? When I am being considered as the commencement speaker at Cardinal MacCauley College, do I not plotz?

By now, I wasn't so hung up on the likelihood that someone more famous and less, as we say, "ethnic" dropped out at the last minute. Hey, maybe they really did want a tribesman this year. Maybe they were trying to broaden their appeal, to think outside the cross. Maybe it was all part of some elaborate PR campaign to reposition themselves, like Abercrombie & Fitch. Remember when that place used to sell argyle socks to the elderly?

Still, it was hard to picture that first brainstorming meeting of the Cardinal MacCauley Commencement Committee.

"Is Jackie Mason available?" Sister Kathleen would ask.

"No, he's doing Brandeis," Monsignor O'Ryan would answer. "Then let's get out there and find ourselves the *next* Jackie Mason!" Sister Kathleen would cheer.

And that is where I'd come into the picture.

I'm not proud to admit that I was playing right into that neurotic Jewish male stereotype, full of insecurity and self-doubt. Was this any way for an inspirational person to behave? No is the answer. The real reason Sister Kathleen was about to call, I assured myself, was because I had a very persuasive agent. A very persuasive agent who talks very, very fast. She must have thought he said "Dan Kevin" instead of Dan Zevin.

I rejoice to announce that Sister Kathleen stated my last name at several junctures throughout our screener, and made the Z sound each and every time. As if that wasn't flattering enough right off the bat, she also said she was confident I'd have a message for her students that was "inspirational-slash-lighthearted." And if she was confident, I guess I was confident.

I liked Sister Kathleen's chutzpah. Midway through our friendly little chitchat, I even found myself flipping through the alumni magazine again, no longer immobilized by the portrait of Rooney Student Center and its dominant architectural feature. This wasn't some strict seminary, I began to see. It felt more like Boston College, for instance, or Notre Dame—one of those campuses that started out a little Jesus-freaky a long time ago, but is now devout only to the extent that everyone gets totally tanked in observance of St. Patrick's Day. Who better to inspire them than me?

Lest she had any last-minute doubts that I wasn't the right Jew for the job, I shifted into maximum assimilation mode to close the deal. This consisted of making repeated references to my wife, who is neither (a) Irish nor (b) Catholic, but is still named (c) Megan, which couldn't hurt. "My wife, MEGAN, to whom I am married, is named MEGAN," I told Sister Kathleen again and again. I also mentioned that the Celtics are my favorite Eastern Conference team. She had to take another call before I got a chance to share fond memories of *The Flying Nun*.

So that was that. All I had to do now was come up with an inspirational-slash-lighthearted message to share with the graduates of Cardinal MacCauley College. By Sunday. At two o'clock.

It was either my third or fourth, or possibly my millionth, draft when it became clear that I had nothing inspirational-slash-lighthearted to share with the graduates of Cardinal MacCauley College by Sunday at two o'clock. They were young and idealistic, full of potential and promise. It was depressing, you know? I don't mean it was depressing that they were young, or idealistic, or full of potential, or promise. I mean it was depressing that I wasn't. Every page of the alumni magazine mocked me with images of carefree youngsters who not only knew how to type a text message, but also knew how to do the hip handshake with the snapping and the clapping; who never had to schedule an organized "date night" with whoever they were hooking up with; who still participated in the practice of brunch. The world was their oyster. The little shits.

Obviously, there was a fine line between inspirational-slash-lighthearted and spiteful-slash-malicious. So that afternoon, I spent some quiet time reflecting upon my own commencement, and the words of wisdom that were surely imparted to *me*. I went to the playroom and dug out a milk crate marked *NYU*, which contained the following memorabilia:

➤ Two (2) empty bottles of Bartles & Jaymes wine cooler (Fuzzy Navel flavor) coated with multicolored candle wax drippings

➤ Three (3) Police cassettes, including *Zenyattà Mondatta,* which I eagerly popped into Josie's Tuff Stuff toddler tape player

➤ One (1) Lucite frame containing a graduation photo of a guy I vaguely remembered as me: a young scholar with a Jewfro stuffed into a commencement cap, his frame draped in a tentlike gown (with no underpants)

Also I unearthed a congratulations card from my father, Dr. Ronald Zevin of Short Hills, New Jersey. The front depicted an earnest grad in cap and gown (and underpants, one presumes). The inside read, and I quote, "Graduate, as you turn the page toward tomorrow, remember: Life is a book of many chapters." I stuck a reminder Post-it note on it: *Send to Kevin MacRae.*

Gazing back on graduation day helped brighten my mood, but only when I cranked up the Tuff Stuff and started rocking out to "De Do Do Do, De Da Da Da." A timeless refrain, it summed up all I had to say to the senior class of Cardinal MacCauley College. There wasn't one thing I could remember about my own graduation day that would shed any light on theirs. It was just another trip down Memory Loss Lane, of which I have taken many in recent years.

Who gave our graduation speech? I e-mailed my old college chum, Doug. (Texting was out of the question.)

I don't remember, came Doug's answer.

Why don't we remember? I wrote back.

Because we were baked, came the reply.

And thus our correspondence was not in vain, as it provided an entirely plausible explanation for my memory impairment.

Subsequent hours of online and in-person procrastination led me to formulate the theory that follows: Not only doesn't anyone remember who spoke at their graduation, they also don't remember anything that person said. The vast majority of those surveyed (three) thought their graduation speaker may have been Bill Cosby. Not a single individual polled could remember what Bill Cosby may have said, however. The closest anyone came was my friend Allen, who went to Stanford, and recalled that Bill Cosby "probably gave us advice."

Finally, the pressure was off! No one was ever going to remember me or a single lighthearted-slash-inspirational word that came out of my mouth! And if they did, they would think Bill Cosby said it. You should have seen my fingers fly across the keyboard that Saturday night.

On Sunday afternoon, the dominant architectural feature of Rooney Student Center shimmered in the sun. It was even bigger and crossier than it looked in the alumni magazine, but once I went inside, I felt more at home. A nice platter of bagels awaited those of us in the VIP area. Even so, I had a feeling I was the lone VJP among them. I say this because my first reaction to the smorgasbord was: *What, no lox?*

Most of the other gentlemen in the VIP area, the youngest of whom I'd put in his early hundreds, were wearing pope suits. Some of the female VIPs were wearing nun dresses, but the ratio of popes to nuns was around 5:1. As for the remaining VIPs, they were all wearing standard-issue graduation gowns, and their "Hello My Name Is" stickers tagged them as Trustees. You know how every so often you'll see a fully grown man or woman walking down the street in a Boy Scout or Girl Scout uniform? That's what the Trustees looked like in their graduation garb. And so did I, at least after Sister Kathleen herself came rushing over with my attire. I recognized her from her picture in the magazine. In person, however, she wore an all-white nun dress, even the hat, which I figured she saved for special occasions.

When I emerged from the VIP bathroom decked out in my cap, gown, and age-appropriate undergarments, Sister Kathleen was waiting excitedly to introduce me to an older couple. I figured they were Trustees, except that only the husband was wearing the graduation garb, and it wasn't black like the others. It was blue, like mine. As a matter of fact, we were the only two people in the room wearing the blue. Were we color-coded?

"Dan Zevin, I'd like you to meet Reuben and Iris Schwartz."

As I stood there shaking the hand of Reuben Schwartz, here is what Sister Kathleen said in the way of an icebreaker: "You two have something in common."

No way, I thought. No way did she drag these two over here because they were the only other Hebrews in Rooney Hall. "Schwartz," I reminded myself, is one of those names that's easily misunderstood. She could have said *Schwarz*, which rhymes with "doors." You know, like FAO Schwarz. When it's *Schwarz* (like doors), it's not Jewish anymore, and no matter how long our people go on saying FAO *Schwartz*—trying to convince ourselves that such a big-shot toy concern can't possibly be goyish—well, guess what? Same with Bruce Springsteen. How we long to claim him as one of our own, and yet. Two *e*'s. Mark Wahlberg, if you're following any of this, is pretty much a switch-hitter, meaning he is or he isn't depending on the quality of his current project. When he was in *The Fighter*, we were all "Wahlberg! A *Jewish* name!" When he was Marky Mark in the Funky Bunch, we preferred to focus on the *h*.

At some point, I realized I'd been shaking the hand of Reuben Schwartz-or-Schwarz for like, ten minutes. Finally, I glanced at his "Hello My Name Is" sticker.

Swirtz.

Swirtz, I didn't know from.

"You and Reuben are both getting honorary degrees this afternoon," Sister Kathleen said, joining our hands. "Thank you both for being such inspirations."

Sister Kathleen went over to talk to one of the pontiffs, leaving me and the Swirtzes to kibitz in the corner. Reuben was a retired professor of public policy who was getting a civic leadership award for making a lasting contribution to the field of social justice. I was at once very impressed and very sure Sister Kathleen was wrong about something: we obviously had *nothing* in common. Actually, it was still possible that there was one thing, but it's not like I was about to go, "So, what kind of name is Swirtz, anyway?"

As luck would have it, Iris answered my question by asking one of her own.

"That's my daughter Marla over there," she said, pointing to a gorgeous young civilian standing alone by the stained-glass window. "You know anyone for her?"

Before I could utter the words *my younger brother, Richie,* the church bells began clanging a deafening rendition of "Pomp and Circumstance." Gathered beneath an enormous white tent, a crowd of four thousand had assembled for commencement exercises. Sister Kathleen threw open the doors of Rooney Student Center, and proudly led me, Reuben, the popes, the nuns, and all the other VIPs in a red-carpet procession straight to center stage. She warmed up the crowd with a little Benediction and Invocation shtick, and the next thing I knew, all eyes were on me.

Life is a book of many chapters, I explained to the promising young grads that afternoon. Turning back the pages to the late 1980s, I myself was a freshly baked bachelor of the arts. But as my story unfolded, I became a husband; a father; a commencement addresser. And now here I was, once more in cap and gown, also underpants, commencing into the next chapter of *my* life. My life as: a doctor.

It is true. I became an honorary Doctor of Humane Letters that day, even though I still don't really know what that is. All I know is I am now a doctor. A Jewish doctor, more importantly—the very *definition* of "inspirational" among my humble tribe. And I owe it all to Kevin MacRae, Sister Kathleen, and Cardinal MacCauley College.

As a wise man once said (I believe it was Bill Cosby), the Lord works in mysterious ways.

Nanny in a Haystack

I used to think nannies were for privileged career couples who enjoyed the convenience of outsourcing their off-spring. Then my wife's maternity leave ended.

This was when Leo was an only child whose parents were conflicted about resuming their regularly scheduled lives. Megan was a little more conflicted than me. This is because she has a little more of a job than me. Okay, not a little. A lot. For instance, her job includes perks like a steady paycheck. Our original plan was for me to transition from stay-at-home writer to stay-at-home dad. Our revised plan, implemented after four days of our original plan, was Stephanie.

Stephanie was twenty-three and had just graduated from art school, which explained not only her hairstyle (green), but also her career path (babysitter). As nannies went, she made it easy to put class consciousness aside. I felt altruistic knowing she was the only one at the playground wearing an Oxfam pin and tutoring underprivileged kids after bringing Leo home from baby yoga. I just wish I could take credit for discovering her. But that distinction belongs to our far hipper next-door neighbors, Max and Kim. They had their baby, Shane, a few months before us, and hired Stephanie after a long search. When Megan's maternity leave ended, they asked if I'd be interested in sharing Stephanie with them a couple of days per week. It was an act of pity, but it made a lot of sense. By chipping in for child care, we'd all spend a little less, Stephanie would earn a little more, and both babies would have a built-in bro. My exhaustive background check consisted of one call to her previous employer, a mother of three in Connecticut who said, "I'm not sure how I'm going to live without her."

So unsure that she elected not to. After one year, she stole her back. There was no way to compete with her offer of a full-time, live-in position, all expenses paid. Stephanie was breaking up with us. The boys would be heartbroken, but they were barely a year old at that point. They had their whole lives to rebound, but me? I wasn't so sure. Not only had Stephanie and I spent every Monday and Thursday of the last year sharing the same place of employment—my town house—but we'd finally reached a comfort level in our new roles. I grew comfortable enough to come downstairs from my study wearing my professional Content Provider's uniform—pajamas stained with Infant Mylanta—and Stephanie grew comfortable enough to arrive at work each morning in her ever-expanding array of hipster nannywear. Elbow-length velvet gloves; miniskirts and go-go boots; an urban cowgirl ensemble featuring pigtails dyed green and blue, respectively. I'm not going to lie to you. It got a little weird there that week with all the bird tattoos. But after a while, I even stopped noticing those. All I noticed was that Leo and his next-door neighbor, Shane, were wild about her. For the first time in months, I could go to my study and polish off a few nauseatingly upbeat posts for OldMan.com (latest blog: "Insomnia: Sleep Less, Accomplish More!"). When I'd come downstairs for coffee, I usually found her bopping around the kitchen with one kid in each arm, leading her daily session of Stephanie's Rock Star Training Camp, as she liked to call it.

I'm still not sure where she unearthed my UB40 tape, but it coincided with the equally unexplained vanishing of the Raffi Singable Songs Collection my mother gave Leo for Hanukkah. Maybe it was just a coincidence. Or maybe Stephanie was teaching our children right from wrong. She really taught them a lot that first year. To this day, I'm convinced Leo learned primary colors so fast thanks to her hair.

She gave two months' notice. That seemed like forever from my point of view, which is the point of view of a guy who has no idea how long it takes to find a nanny since his next-door neighbors did all the work the first time around. This time, though, both couples would be in on the search, convening on weekends to conduct group interviews. It was a logical plan, and one that quickly illuminated why my wife was the one with the real job in the real office with the real staff, and I was the one working upstairs in pajamas stained with Infant Mylanta. She was like a research scientist, e-mailing me a daily directory of referrals, web sites, and professional groups such as the International Nanny Association (INA), which appeared to be the William Morris Endeavor of child-care talent. I didn't follow up on several to all of her leads. But that didn't mean I wasn't pulling my weight, I assured her. We just had different staffing styles. I took a grassroots approach, eagerly hitting the street with a word-of-mouth campaign. My to-do list became a model of multitasking: "Get applesauce (and nanny)"; "Drop off dry-cleaning (pick up nanny)"; "Tony's Hardware (Tony's daughter?)" I never returned without prospects. For one thing, our neighborhood is lousy with privileged career couples who enjoy the convenience of outsourcing their offspring. For another, our neighborhood is in Brooklyn, where it is the civic duty of citizens to tell each other what they should do.

"You have *got* to call Anling, she is the best, best, best," commanded a mom named Paige I met one morning while walking our dog (and finding our nanny). Now that Paige's kids were in school, she no longer needed Anling. She called us that night, raving about how the tireless Anling took her kids all over town when they were Leo's age—parks, aquariums, museums. The museum thing, incidentally, was something I'd hear again and again from parents. It seemed like a real feather in your cap to land a nanny who took your baby to museums. I didn't really see what was in it for a preschooler, so I figured I'd find out one day. I selected the Guggenheim, because I remembered from a junior high field trip that it didn't have stairs. It was like a giant spiral in there, perfect for the stroller-bound patron of the arts. After schlepping Leo all the way uptown on the subway, changing his nasty diaper on the even nastier floor of a Taco Bell men's room, then sprinting him down Fifth Avenue because it was the only way to get him to stop screaming in his stroller, we finally got to the museum's ticket counter—which is where they display the sign that says "No Strollers."

I asked Paige if there was anything else I should know before calling Anling for an interview.

"Nope," she said. "It's not important to you that she gets English, right?"

I paused. "Well, maybe not perfectly, but—"

"Good, because Anling doesn't get English. We loved that about her."

I guess I could have asked what, specifically, it was that they loved about Anling's not getting English, but it just seemed like too much to tackle at that point.

"She speaks Mandarin Chinese," Paige said, with pride. "I'm sure you know it's going to be the most widely used language in the world by the time our kids are grown. Don't you?"

She went on to boast that *muchin* was one of her daughter's first words. I tried to be tactful.

"But what if there was ever an emergency situation? How would she be able to explain what was wrong?"

"Oh, you new dads!" said Paige, laughing at me. "With Anling, there won't ever *be* an emergency situation!"

I would like to note at this point that any New Yorker who can state unequivocally that "there won't ever be an emergency situation" has crossed a line from cockeyed optimism to blind denial. Even with Stephanie, who really *was* the best, best, best, there was once an emergency situation. She rushed upstairs to my study one morning in a panic, pointing to her face. The tiny gold ball bearing from her nose stud fell off, she explained, leaving a sharp tip protruding from her left nostril. Naturally, she was worried that it could scratch Leo or Shane, so we spent the next fifteen minutes scouring the living room rug the way normal people might look for a contact lens. The nose stud never materialized, but she improvised by screwing on an earring back she found in Megan's jewelry box. She felt it was safer than covering it with the decorative gem I'd fashioned out of Play-Doh. And, thus, danger was narrowly averted.

Still, one had to wonder. What if it was Anling whose nose stud unexpectedly disattached one day? How would she be able to explain it to me in a calm, non-Mandarin manner? Or might she, like her smug former employer, Paige, simply choose to believe that "there won't ever be an emergency situation"? One minute she'd be sniffing around Leo's Pampers, the next, we'd have to get her nose surgically removed from his ass.

"Sorry, it's kind of a deal-breaker that she doesn't get English," I told Paige before hanging up.

A couple of weeks into the search, I realized that *everyone* thought their nanny was the best, best, best. Even Steve from Bergen Street, whose nanny I personally witnessed falling asleep one afternoon at Café Boobah. Leo and I used to hang out there sometimes when it rained. It was a cross between a Gymboree and a Starbucks, brilliantly serving the dual needs of babies and their caregivers. Apparently, Steve's nanny ordered decaf that day. She was leaning against the Velcro wall, watching Steve's kid stick the felt bumblebees on it. She yawned, then just . . . shut her eyes. Seriously. She was still standing. The coffee girl had to go wake her up. And it wasn't easy, either. I think it was the loud ripping noise of her sweater against the Velcro wall that finally did the trick.

"The thing I love about our nanny is she's incredibly energetic," Steve told me the following week. I happened to see him walk by as I was engaged in my daily ritual of driving my minivan around in search of a legal parking spot (and a legal nanny). Steve and his wife were thrilled when his nanny said she took their kid to a museum when it rained the other day. I had to break the news. Maybe what she meant to say, I suggested, was that she woke up from a dream in which she took their kid to a museum.

She is still under their employ.

A few days later, a flyer on a phone pole urged me to "Please Help Our Creative, Resourceful Nanny Find a New Family." I called the number and spoke to a busy executive who was leaving her advertising career to become a stay-at-home mom. About the creative, resourceful nanny, she said (as a compliment), "To be honest, I don't even know what she does with my kids all day."

I found out when the creative, resourceful nanny returned

my call later that day. At first, I thought we had a bad connection, but she explained it was just *E! News* blaring on TV in the background. "These kids like it really loud," was how the creative, resourceful nanny put it.

And so it was that I disregarded all references and went straight to the source. The Prospect Park playground was crawling with caregivers, and the possibilities for recruiting—some might say "stealing"—seemed limitless. Leo and I became regulars, and soon familiarized ourselves with three distinct categories:

1. pack nannies
2. English major nannies
3. Dionne

Dionne was the category best suited to our needs. She was fun and affectionate and I admired her chlorine-free wipes. She agreed to an informational interview I conducted in the sandbox. Everything was going great until I asked if she was happily employed and she provided the incorrect answer ("yes").

She did tip me off to her cousin Bernadette, though. She was also a nanny, Dionne said, and she might be in the market for a new situation. I found myself fantasizing about this cousin Bernadette in days to come. Cousin Bernadette, who "got" English. Cousin Bernadette, who would not fall asleep on the Velcro wall. Cousin Bernadette, who would take Leo to museums. *That nanny over there seems pretty good*, I'd find myself thinking as I stalked some random sitter by the twisty slide. *But she's no Cousin Bernadette.*

I slipped Dionne my cell phone number and she promised to pass it along.

While awaiting the coming of Cousin Bernadette, Leo and I agreed to eliminate category one (pack nannies). As we observed from our fieldwork, pack nannies shoved their strollers down the sidewalk in herds of three or four wide, headed for any park bench big enough to fit them all while the kids wandered off one by one, only to reappear later on milk cartons asking, "Have you seen this child?"

We settled instead on category two (English major nannies) as our Cousin Bernadette backup plan. For starters, it seemed safe to assume that English majors would "get" English. Not only that, but they could also help *Leo* get it—a major perk considering my wife and I lost our own ability to form full sentences shortly after his birth.

That Saturday afternoon, I went by myself to the NYU library to check out some books (and nannies). No, I wasn't checking them out the way that last sentence sounded. Yes, I had a tough time convincing a few co-eds of that, too. I subsequently learned to do my campus recruiting only when Leo was actually *with* me.

Our next-door neighbor Kim called a few days later. She wanted to make sure Megan and I could come over the following weekend to meet some candidates she and her husband found on craigslist. Yes, I told her, of course we could come. We were planning on it. We could barely wait. I then placed a call to my wife at her office in midtown Manhattan.

"Do you think it's a good idea to find a nanny on craigslist?"

"Sure, why not?"

"I don't know. Doesn't it seem a little random?"

"Dan, you've been picking up nannies at the playground."

"I'm not picking them up. I'm screening them."

Megan went off to a meeting, and I went on to discover a level of procrastination known only to those who've lost all contact with the outside world. I've never been completely clear on who this Craig is, but let me tell you something. The guy really has an outstanding list. Over the next two hours, I found face-value Mets tickets *and* a pair of twenty-pound dumbbells I last lifted on the afternoon I picked them up from the guy's apartment.

Also, I spent several intensive seconds screening all the ads posted by nannies. One in particular caught my attention immediately. "Does Johnny Have Two Mommies?" the headline inquired. "Then I'm Your Manny!" It was placed by a normal-sounding guy in his twenties, aimed at gay mothers looking for a male role model who'd teach their sons about sports and power tools. Now, I'm no lesbian, but frankly, this fella sounded pretty good. I decided to give him a break, figuring he wasn't about to be inundated with other offers. His answering machine informed me that he'd already accepted a position.

On Saturday morning, Megan dressed Leo in his cutest baby costume (the onesie that says "rock star in training," which Stephanie gave him) and we went next door to Max and Kim's. As far as Leo and Shane knew, they were just going to hang out and crawl around, unaware that they were mere props for the pageant of hopefuls who'd be auditioning for the part of their nanny. I still remember the first one who showed up. She carried a clipboard and passed out copies of her résumé, then crossed her legs on the couch like someone sent over from HR. Midway through the interview, she still hadn't acknowledged the children. At one point, Leo even put his hands on her knees and propped himself up. She hardly looked down. He waved his hands around her eyes. She soldiered on. I swear, if the kid smacked her in the head and shouted, "Snap out of it!" it wouldn't have mattered. She was a "Seen One, Seen 'Em All" nanny; one of many we'd meet who somehow didn't understand that our children were special—the first of their species to show us their belly buttons, for example, or pull out their pacifiers all by themselves.

Subsequent Saturdays played out like a bad movie montage where the door slams shut on a series of oddball character actors. There was the one who lit a cigarette and blew smoke rings to entertain the kids; the one who sang the alphabet song wrong (Q-R-X-T-U-V); the one in the tank top with sparkly letters that spelled *Jamaican Girls Love to Party*. She spent a solid ten minutes outlining her job demands, including that we stock bammy bread in the fridge for her lunch. I had no clue what bammy bread was, but figured I could find a loaf on craigslist if I ever hit rock bottom.

I hit rock bottom the day I wished Leo had a developmental disability. It was during our interview with an earnest Midwesterner who had a Masters in pediatric psychology. Her name was Mary Pat, and she recently moved from Wisconsin because her fiancé got into dental school uptown. Ideally, Mary Pat wanted to be a creative arts counselor at a facility for developmentally disabled youth, but after an unsuccessful job search, she decided to explore "direct service." That was Mary Pat's way of saying "nanny." Throughout her interview, she sprinkled in references to "social behavior deficits," "imitative play," "facilitated communication." It was all a little touchy-feely, but it wasn't Mandarin, and we weren't in a position to be picky anymore. Mary Pat was our top choice.

But we weren't hers. She was still waiting to hear back about one last position, as a "dance therapist" at a group home for adolescents with severe developmental disabilities. She described it as her dream job.

"Well, *that's* funny, because *Leo* loves to dance," I remarked, praying that Megan, Kim, and Max would take my lead.

"Oh. Yeah, so does Shane," Max chimed in. He put "Sweetest Thing" on his iPod and the kids swayed back and forth to Bono, shaking mini maracas. A grin came over Mary Pat as she watched. She was charmed. All I had to do now was convince her they were developmentally disabled.

Leo beat me to it by making Crazy Face. Reflecting back on his first year of life, I would have to say Crazy Face was his original tour de force. It entailed raising both eyebrows, opening his mouth, and rapidly shaking his head in a convulsive fashion while giggling. I hoped Mary Pat would interpret Crazy Face as the face of a child who was not merely being silly, but being developmentally disabled. Would it be wrong to go ahead and suggest it to her myself, I wondered? What if I added that he has dyslexia or something like that to sweeten the deal? I could always tell her it cleared up on its own, like pimples, when she showed up for her first day of direct service.

Leo wrapped up with Crazy Face.

"Wow, he has a terrific sense of humor," said Mary Pat, to my great disappointment.

She called several days later to say she was offered the job at the developmentally disabled place. I thought she was just being her polite, Wisconsiny self when she went on to say that choosing between us and them was one of the hardest decisions of her life, but Crazy Face apparently left quite an impression. Mary Pat was torn. Was there anything else I could tell her, she asked, that might help make up her mind? I thought about it, but what was I going to say? That she'd be nuts to take the job she spent her whole education preparing for? The one that not only paid more, but came with health insurance and colleagues and challenging case-study kids whose lives she could "impact," to use one of her favorite verbs? Nah, even I couldn't bring myself to convince her she'd be happier wiping tushies all day. The best I could do was suggest she spend an afternoon shadowing Stephanie, to see for herself how she'd like working for us. I also may have mentioned an article I read in the *Times* about gang violence in the vicinity of the developmentally disabled place.

Later that day, I went downstairs for more coffee. Stephanie was wearing a yellow hard hat. She'd asked a local construction worker if she could borrow it to play "Bob the Builder," and he obliged very enthusiastically. Now here she was on the floor with Leo and Shane, rolling a tiny dump truck up and down the hall as they watched in amazement. I wanted to get on my knees and beg her to stay. If it was a live-in job she needed, she could live with us. We had an air mattress in the basement. We could prop it up with bricks so she wouldn't get wet if the cement floor flooded again.

Stephanie adjusted her hard hat and informed me that she had to leave one week earlier than expected because her new family was going to Rome on vacation and they wanted her to come. I made a mental note: check craigslist for bammy bread.

One thing you should know about me and Megan is that we don't fight. We discuss. Sometimes it might sound like we're fighting, but we're not. We're just discussing, loudly. That evening, the topic of our discussion was "What If We Don't Find a Nanny by Friday?" You probably heard us.

Just to jog your memory, our discussion commenced when Megan decided she should quit her job, and I replied that we couldn't afford to live in New York without her job. Okay, she said, let's move to the suburbs. *The suburbs?* I said. What museums would Leo go to?

No, the only realistic option was for me to pack in the writing game and become a full-time stay-at-home dad. After all, I was already a part-time stay-at-home dad, and the only reason I was doing it part-time instead of full-time was . . . what, exactly? The answer was: selfishness. Megan assured me I was being too hard on myself. Only *women* are considered selfish for trying to combine work and parenthood, she noted, which of course was true, and which led to my brilliant solution that we *both* stop working, so we could *both* stay home with Leo all day. We could start our own business together! We could run it from our house!

"So . . . who's going to watch Leo all day while we're both running our own business from our house?" Megan asked.

"What's the big deal?" I said. "We'll just get a nanny to come in a couple days a week."

It was right about there that our discussion went up a few decibels. It came to a deafening silence when I blurted out that I wouldn't want to start a business with her anyway because that pencil thing she does when she's on the phone would drive me insane—that way she always has to tap it on her desk when she talks.

I regretted my words immediately. And in that moment, I finally understood what had to be done.

Cousin Bernadette cheerfully took me up on my offer to put twenty bucks in her pocket just for stopping by to meet the boys. She didn't look a whole lot like I'd envisioned, but then again I'd packed on a few pounds myself, so who was I to judge? As soon as she sang the ABC song (accurately) (in English), all four parents fell in love. We couldn't let it go unrequited.

"Anguilla? No way!" I gushed when she told us where she

grew up. "We *love* the Bahamas!" Anguilla, as it turns out, is not a Bahama. Yet Cousin Bernadette knew I was just trying to make her feel like part of our family. Or, to be succinct, more like part of *our* family than part of the one that currently employed her. She kept referring to them as "famous celebrities." Famous celebrities who were moving to "Hollywood, California." They begged her to go with them, but she wasn't sure about leaving New York. All parties present strongly agreed with her reluctance. One party may also have mentioned an article he read in the *Times* about gang violence in the vicinity of Hollywood, California.

The thing is, Cousin Bernadette explained, these two are *famous celebrities*, so we couldn't call them for a reference. As an alternative, she promised us a letter of reference. A letter of reference from the famous celebrities.

"Sarah Jessica Parker and Matthew Broderick," our friend Judy guessed when we told her the story. "What other famous celebrities live in New York and have kids?"

"Uma Thurman and Ethan Hawke!" insisted Megan's cousin, which we discounted immediately because they'd long since split, and Cousin Bernadette specifically said famous celebri*ties*, plural, so it wasn't like she was talking about a single-parent famous celebrity.

"Listen to what I'm telling you: Rosie O'Donnell and Melissa Etheridge." This last pick was phoned in from New Jersey by my mother, aka Grandma Linda. She was receiving a pedicure and rifling through *InStyle* magazine at the time. "Laugh all you want, Daniel, but if you knew anything about famous celebrities, you'd know the two of them are gay lesbian mothers." I freely admitted that I don't know anything about famous celebrities. From what little I did know, however, the two of them weren't gay lesbian mothers *together*. And if they were, they would never have hired Cousin Bernadette. They would have hired that manny from craigslist.

Finally, the letter of reference arrived in the mail, with no return address. It was a handwritten note on dainty rose-colored stationery. The O'Donnell-Etheridges were out of the running.

"Dear perspective parents . . ."

Perspective? I thought to myself. Whatever. They're famous celebrities, they don't have time to proofread.

"She was patient and loving with our daughter, namely Lisa."

Namely? Who says "namely"? Who does that? And Lisa? What happened to Apple, or Phinneus? Or Scout LaRue?

"And she always had something fun planned, such as a trip to the museum."

Here we go with the museums. . . .

"Best wishes, E. Moran."

E. Moran? Who the fuck is E. Moran??

"The chick who played Richie's sister on *Happy Days*! Erin Moran!" answered my old chum Doug, who has a remarkable capacity to remember these things. Megan came home from work just as he was reminiscing about the one where she joins Pinky Tuscadero's band. I handed her the letter of reference. It was quickly transformed into a crumpled-up ball she tossed over her shoulder.

"Wack job," stated Megan. "She wrote it herself."

I was inclined to agree, but felt we owed her one last chance. I called her up while Megan read a bedtime story to our son, namely Leo. Wasn't there any way, I asked Cousin Bernadette, that we could talk to her current employers?

"I'm sorry," she said, "but you know how it is. They're—"

"Famous celebrities, yeah, I know."

"But if there's anything I can add to the letter they wrote, just let me know."

I took a moment to consider my next move.

"Well, I've gotta say I was glad to read that you take Lisa to museums."

"Yes, I *love* taking her to museums."

"You know which museum I like taking Leo to?" I continued. "The Guggenheim. It's so perfect for strollers, ya know?"

"Of course!" Cousin Bernadette exclaimed. "That's what I love about it, too!"

Mary Pat arrived for job-shadowing day just as I was looking for more Mets tickets (and nannies) on craigslist. Just as she'd promised, she'd come to compare a typical day at our place to a typical day at the developmentally disabled place, hoping the experience would help her decide where she'd be happier. I'd already prepped Stephanie to lay it on thick, so I was pleased to find her extolling our brand-new Diaper Genie when I came downstairs from my study. Still, there was a part of me that wasn't 100 percent comfortable knowing that Leo was just one of two choices for Mary Pat. I wanted him to be the only choice. Like everyone else who ever hired a nanny, Megan and I wanted the best, best, best. Three months later, we were resigned to take someone who wasn't the worst, worst, worst. We told ourselves it was only two days a week, for God's sake. If Mary Pat would settle for us, we would settle for Mary Pat.

Which is why you may find it peculiar that I issued the following directive to Stephanie shortly after returning to my desk upstairs: "You have to get rid of Mary Pat." Understandably, Stephanie was confused, partly by my reversal and partly because she'd never gotten a phone call from me when I was upstairs and she was downstairs.

"Yes-or-no question—Is Mary Pat right next to you?" I whispered into the phone.

"Yes."

I told her to act nonchalant as I detailed a late-breaking development. Megan was rushing home on her lunch hour to meet a nanny she found on something called Care.net just this morning. She already talked to her on the phone (in English) and she sounded perfect. She was interning at a preschool a few days per week. She was CPR-certified. She coached a kids' soccer team back where she grew up, in Grenada (not a Bahama, I was sternly informed). And right now, before someone else drafted her, Megan wanted her to meet the boys. Who were here. At our house. With Mary Pat.

"What am I supposed to do with her?" Stephanie nonchalantly muttered into her cell phone.

"I don't know, go for a walk."

Stephanie loaded up the double stroller—the limo, as she used to call it—and ushered the group out for a little fresh air. When she returned with the boys (having stuffed Mary Pat into a cab back home), Megan and I were sitting in the living room with our next-door neighbors, Kim and Max, silently waiting for Possibly Perfect Part-Time Nanny. Who blew us off.

But you want to know something? It didn't matter. It motivated me, as a matter of fact. It was just the catalyst I needed to step up to the plate and start raising my own son instead of farming him out to a freelancer.

Several years have passed since then, and it's funny how a parent's perspective can change. Now we have two kids, Leo and Josephine, and I wouldn't even consider leaving them with some possibly perfect part-time nanny. I'm holding out for a totally perfect, full-time au pair.

Mommy and Me

My mother's coccyx is killing her. "It's either a fracture or a contusion, I can't decide," she announced this morning, shuffling through my front door with an exaggerated limp. "I hope you don't plan on going anywhere, because my two favorite grandchildren will be needing us both today."

As usual, I was planning to go somewhere; somewhere important, as a matter of fact. I had a date with my laptop at the Flying Saucer Café, where I planned to finish (and start) my OldMan.com blog in the fourteen minutes remaining before it was due. This week's topic was even more nauseatingly upbeat than usual: "Sexperts Agree: Less Is More!"

I asked my mother how she got a fracture (or possibly a contusion) on her coccyx.

"Dance class," she replied. She takes Intermediate Ballroom and Swing with her boyfriend, Bob, at the Arthur Murray Dance Studio on Route 22. It seems she was in the middle of a fox-trot promenade when all of a sudden she got dizzy and fell flat on her coccyx.

"Boy, he must have spun you around pretty fast," I said.

"Daniel, please. Bob could be the next Baryshnikov. Which you'd know if you ever came to watch us dance."

It is a delicate balance of pros and cons, these weekly visits from my mother. The good part is that she wants to spend time with the kids. The bad part is that I'm one of the kids she wants to spend time with. Like a hurricane, she blows in from New Jersey each Tuesday, with freshly manicured fingernails and a dazzling assortment of suitcase-size pocketbooks. Leo and Josie wait by the door because they're crazy about her, and they know she comes bearing toys. I wait by the door because I'm planning a swift exit, and I know these toys always have names like "A Trillion Tiny Pieces That Need to Be Connected." Every Tuesday, they're presented with the same familiar fanfare.

"We're gonna have a ball playing with this today!" Grandma Linda will tell Leo and Josie. "Just as soon as Daddy figures out how to put it together."

As a guy with a working wife, there is much to be gained from her grandmotherly services. Offspring will be cleansed; pajamas will be folded; meatballs will be made. But so will demands. Subtle—and not so subtle—demands of intergenerational togetherness, which can get tricky if you're a grown man who, say, can't get his work done because his mother wants to chat about her coccyx.

"So why did you get dizzy if Bob didn't spin you around too fast?"

"Why did I get dizzy? Why do you think I got dizzy? Because I have Ménière's disease."

Ménière's disease was when it was clear I'd be going to the Flying Saucer Café some other day. Today I'd be going to the living room, where the kids would watch me connect a trillion tiny pieces and my mother would rest her coccyx on a reclining, swiveling chair. She lowered her voice when I asked what Ménière's disease was. Presumably, this was to protect the children.

"It happens to be a very serious condition of the inner ear," she whispered directly into my own. "It's caused by a virus—actually, an *ultravirus*."

I couldn't help but appreciate "ultravirus," surely a self-coined strain explaining a self-diagnosed disease. One of the things I find most endearing about my mother is her ability to get sicker than anyone else. Since we started our Tuesday routine, she has never once called in sick with a cold, but has been a repeat victim of "irritated mucus membranes." A stomachache is salmonella; a freckle, melanoma. In the past calendar year, she's had dry eye, trigger thumb, and trench foot. Plus a spasm. A few Tuesdays ago, she got malaria. It was from one of the mosquitoes swarming by our front door. She seemed to know exactly which one. When it comes to her symptoms, I try not to play favorites, but let me just say this: she's sure she has something called radiculitis.

My mother is not a hypochondriac. That would mean she's strictly concerned with herself. But, with each passing Tuesday, I'm reminded how generous she can be in dispensing her medical expertise to others.

"How's that cute wife of yours?" she'll casually ask.

"Good," I'll say.

"Allergies still bothering her?"

"Yeah," I'll say. "She took a Claritin."

"Did it help?"

"Not really."

"I don't think it's allergies."

"What do you think it is?"

"Legionnaires' disease."

There is not a doubt in my mind that my mother's true calling is infectious diseases. But her field of specialty wouldn't be the diseases themselves. It would be the people she could blame for spreading them. She could be the world's first prosecuting physician.

"I've had cholera all morning. I'm positive that skinny waitress gave it to me last night."

"Josephine just sneezed! I bet it was that baby who touched her rake in the sandbox."

"Chloe, why are you licking your tail like that? Did that schnauzer next door give you tapeworm?"

As an adult, I get a kick out of her bedside manner, but at some point each week, I'll experience one of my Tuesday-afternoon flashbacks. I'll just be sitting there watching her disinfect my daughter with Purell or examine my son's scalp for scabies, and *boom*—I'm right back in 1976. It was the year of our nation's Bicentennial, and I spent every moment of it scratching my testicles. I scratched them in the morning, I scratched them in the evening, I scratched them all year long. I had the itchiest jock in the history of jock itch. But my mother had her own prognosis, which she elected to share at our Passover Seder that year.

"Enough already, Daniel!" she yelled clear across the table I'd been scratching under since sundown. "Has someone given you VD?!"

This was not one of the four questions, so I chose not to answer. Instead, I sat there thinking, *VD? Yeah, I should be so lucky.*

A few Tuesdays later, my mother said she couldn't get to Brooklyn until four o'clock because the girl who does her toenails was extremely backed up. By the time she got through the Holland Tunnel, it was 4:30, and I was still shaky from my inaugural visit to Chuck E. Cheese's. I swore I'd never take the kids to that establishment, but it was a losing battle once they started advertising on PBS KIDS. Josie climbed out of her stroller and wandered off while Leo and I were getting more tokens. I muscled past the throngs of toddlers waiting to get into the scary glass cage with all the balls, and found her inside the Skytube, enjoying a delicious piece of pepperoni she found on the floor.

My mother and her toes got to my house at five. "You look like you need a break," she remarked, accurately. "Would you and Megan like to go out tonight?"

I gave her a hug.

"Wonderful," she said. "I'll get the kids cleaned up, and when she gets home from work, you'll take us all out to that new fish-and-chips place around the corner."

One Tuesday in November, I drove the kids to my mother's house in New Jersey and we went to the Short Hills Mall. It was her idea, if you were wondering. She phoned it in at 6 a.m., jolting me and Megan out of bed.

"It's too nasty out for me to schlep into Brooklyn, as I'm sure you've noticed," she said. I mustered all my eyelid strength to focus on the rain outside our bedroom window.

"So. How about bringing the kids to me for a change? You can take your laptop and write in your old bedroom after you drop us off."

"Drop you off where?" I asked.

"The mall. It'll be fun."

"Why will that be fun?"

"I've got a bunch of stuff to return. They'll have a ball."

Though you may wonder how returning merchandise to the mall could possibly be fun for children—or for any living organism at any stage of its life cycle—one thing I've always admired about my mother is her genuine joy of returning. Even way back when she'd bring me, my brother, and my sister to the Short Hills Mall (on an average of seven nights a week), buying stuff was always just half the transaction. The other half was bringing it all back to request a refund, rebate, exchange, exemption, credit, coupon, voucher, prize, certificate, explanation, apology, and/or affidavit. Mortified, my siblings and I would wait by the entrance, but she actually never made a scene. She'd just take the managers aside and inform them—for their own benefit, really—that the numbers on the clock radio were too blurry, or the Lucite salad tongs were not, in fact, dishwasher-safe. All these years later, my embarrassment has turned into respect. I tried to return Leo's coat to the store the other day because the zipper was busted. Within five minutes, I was fighting with the saleslady. I gave up when she said I should take better care of my children's clothes.

My mother never gives up. It's a trait that continues to impress me. Even as I drove her and the kids to the Short Hills Mall that morning, she whipped out her cell phone and began working her returning mojo on a customer service representative. It goes without saying that she knew her confirmation number. She always does. It's part of her gift.

"Good afternoon, this is Linda Zevin, confirmation number four six eight dash Y-Yellow, B-Boy, V-Victor. And to whom am I talking please? Oh hello, Sanghita, what a pretty name and how are you today? And is the weather in New Delhi as nasty as it is here in New Jersey? Oh, are *you* a lucky one. Now, listen, Sanghita . . ."

By the time we pulled into the parking lot, she had herself a new Melitta coffee machine—the original of which was free in the first place with the purchase of one can of Breakfast

Blend. Her grievance was that the coffee machine was a darker shade of red than the one in the *Parade* magazine ad. Sanghita agreed 100 percent that she deserved another one.

I dropped them off near Macy's because I remembered there was a big glass fountain there that the kids could throw pennies in. This would put them in a good mood for the first ten minutes, I instructed my mother. After that, she should con them with a cookie from Mrs. Fields so they'd cooperate when it came time to return the free samples of eye cream to the Clinique counter.

"Stop having a nervous breakdown, Daniel. You're gonna get an ulcer," is what my mother said.

I couldn't help but wonder: Why not an ultra-ulcer?

"Now go home and write your report already." That's what she calls my blogs for OldMan.com. Reports. Like I'm still in third grade doing reports on kangaroos and Eskimos. Which were actually harder.

I kissed the kids good-bye and said I'd pick them up two hours later.

Two minutes later:

"Daniel, you have to come back to the mall."

"Come on, Ma, I'm not even at your house yet, why are you calling me already?"

"Josie made a caca in Neiman Marcus."

"So? Change her diaper."

"I can't."

"Why can't you?"

"You didn't give me diapers."

"They're in the diaper bag."

"You didn't give me the diaper bag."

"I did so. I handed it to you in the minivan when you were on the phone with Sanghita."

"Well, maybe you handed it to me, but you didn't remind me to take it."

At some earlier era of my life, I would have continued this conversation. But now I knew. I knew not to remind her that there was a CVS in the mall where she could buy diapers because I knew she probably tried that already, and I knew she probably discovered the CVS only had pull-up diapers, or Huggies instead of Pampers, or diapers with trucks instead of princesses. On top of that, I knew she probably bought the truck ones before analyzing them more thoroughly and realizing they were trucks. And if there was one thing I absolutely knew, it was that she'd be returning the truck diapers the next time she went to the CVS at the Short Hills Mall.

"Sorry I forgot the diaper bag, Ma," I said. "I've been really absentminded lately."

My mother graciously accepted my apology. She also suggested bringing my laptop to the mall along with the diaper bag, as a time-saving measure. Evidently, there was some café near Foot Locker she thought would be perfect for writing my report. "You'll love it," is what my mother said. "It's *funky.*"

I changed Josie's diaper in the bathroom of Johnny Rockets, the funky café—"funky" in this case meaning a faux '50s diner franchise mobbed with toddlers who don't even belong to you. I put on my noise-canceling headphones and settled into a red vinyl booth. Grandma Linda, meanwhile, took the kids to The Body Shop to exchange some kind of bath salts my sister gave her fifteen birthdays ago.

For my blog that week, my editor at OldMan.com wanted me to write something nauseatingly upbeat about knee replacement surgery. I'd gotten as far as the headline ("The All-New, Bionic You!"), when who should come fox-trotting back into Johnny Rockets but Grandma Linda, Leo, and Josie.

Josie in particular reeked of whatever vanilla-banana cream rinse they'd slathered all over each other at The Body Shop.

"Surprise, Daddy! We came to have dessert with you!" said Leo, hopping on my lap.

"I wanted to give you enough time to finish your report," added my mother. I waited for her to finish her sentence. Maybe she was going to say, "I wanted to give you enough time to finish your report, but the kids were getting too hungry," or, "I wanted to give you enough time to finish your report, but they really wanted to surprise you." As I waited for her to finish her sentence, though, the thing I realized was that she had, in fact, finished her sentence.

"Thanks, Mom. I appreciate it."

"You're welcome sweetie, lunch is on me! Now let's just change tables because the draft over here is gonna give us all pneumonia."

It took a few years of Grandma Linda Tuesdays before I learned to accept their natural cycle. The cycle begins with me appreciating all her help; recognizing the relationship she's built with the kids; empathically assuring her that you can't actually "catch" epilepsy. The cycle ends with me wanting to kill her again. At these points in the cycle, I find it useful to conduct a Tuesday-night venting session with Megan (who, luckily for me, has staved off the Legionnaires' disease all these years). One of our most memorable sessions occurred late one Tuesday night when we were cleaning up the kitchen after my mother drove her Lexus back to Short Hills. She made meatballs as usual that afternoon. It was supposed to be a cooking project with the kids, but she kept yelling to me in my study upstairs.

"Daniel! Why don't you have any kosher salt?

"Daniel! Come down and help me reach the frying pan!

"Daniel! I need you to run around the corner and get bread crumbs. *Panko*, Daniel! Not regular."

Is it asking too much, I vented to Megan, for one single Tuesday where she'll let me go upstairs, close my door, and write my blog?

Megan stopped loading the dishwasher and looked at me for a second.

"Ya know," she said, "one day *I'm* gonna be a grandma."

This was weird. She's a hottie, Megan. Even in her orange dishwashing gloves.

"It's true," she continued. "One day Leo will probably have kids."

Also weird. He's very young, Leo. I was just grateful she was leaving Josie out of this.

I asked her to stop weirding me out and get to the point.

"It's just that when I'm a grandma and I visit Leo's kids, it would make me really sad if he went upstairs and shut his door until dinner was ready."

"But Leo's gonna be a grown man by that point!" I said, now weirding my own self out. "Why should he spend all day with his mother?"

"Because he's going to be a mensch," she replied, playfully pinching my coccyx with her dishwashing glove. "Just like his dad."

Sometimes it takes a good pinch in the coccyx to get straightened out. At least, that's how Tuesdays turned around for me. No longer do I view them as the day my mother watches the kids so I can go write my blog. Blog Shmog, is what I say now, for Grandma Linda is coming to town! A few Tuesdays ago, I had the privilege of watching my children dress her up as Batgirl. On a separate occasion, I was lucky enough to wit-

ness the three of them bouncing together on the mini trampoline in the kitchen. I've seen her risk nail chippage in order
to finger-paint; I've watched her play kickball with no fear of
grass stains. And on an unseasonably warm Tuesday not long
ago, I took the kids to see her in Bradley Beach, New Jersey,
where she and Baryshnikov share a condo.

When I was little, we spent every summer in Bradley Beach,
and my mother has the faded Polaroids to prove it. They're
still stuck to her fridge with novelty magnets from the same
epoch—Ziggys, Kitchen Witches, you get the picture. Josie
goes crazy for the magnets, but on this particular Tuesday, she
was more interested in one of the photos. In it, a tan, attractive woman in her twenties is standing by the ocean in a yellow bikini, her long brown hair parted down the middle. In
one hand, she's holding a pink can of Tab. In the other, she's
holding an extremely adorable little kid. If I do say so myself.

"That's Daddy, and that's Grandma Linda," I told Josie that
afternoon. She was perplexed—unable to fathom how *those* two
people could possibly turn into *these* two people: an old lady
wearing a floral, Grandma-size bathing suit–skirt thing, and a
goofy daddy whose iPod contains not one but two different ver-
sions of "Head, Shoulders, Knees, and Toes (Knees and Toes)."

The two of us knelt down to Josie's level and took a closer
look at the photo on the fridge.

"Ma," I said to her, "when was this picture taken?"

"Yesterday," she said with a sigh. "Oh my God did you grow
up fast."

It was a touching moment of intergenerational togetherness, and as she turned her gaze from the faded snapshot to
me, I'll never forget what my mother said next.

"Why is your T-zone so irritated like that? That looks like
rosacea, you know."

Dating Ourselves

I.

"ыкзкя зуденан иякиар руссй"

This is the phrase that springs to mind when I think back to my first date with Megan. Loosely translated from Russian, it means, "Perhaps you two would like private cabin?" We were a couple of crazy, Eurail Pass–carrying college kids taking a night train to Moscow. Immersed in our heavy petting activities, we failed to note the existence of our fellow passengers, in addition to the Eastern Bloc rushing past our window.

We'd known each other about a month, since Orientation Day at the University of Copenhagen. We were both taking a semester abroad. I was a suburban schlemiel in a Chaps flannel shirt. The closest I'd ever come to world travel was the International House of Pancakes. When it was time for the class to take turns introducing ourselves, Megan said she was born near San Francisco, spent her childhood in Paris, her teen years in New England, and chose to study here in Denmark because she'd recently ended a serious relationship that was interfering with her thesis on Scandinavian literature. She was the sexiest girl—no, *woman*—I'd ever seen. Traveling a kajillion miles to recover from a serious relationship? The most serious relationship I myself had experienced at that juncture began after an AEΠ toga party and lasted approximately three minutes before meeting its, shall we say, "premature" conclusion.

"I picked Denmark in order to continue my research on Tuborg beer," I remarked when it was my turn to share. "Back at NYU, I had the largest Tuborg pyramid on any windowsill in Rubin Hall."

From the corner of my eye, I saw Megan half-laugh, like she couldn't tell if I was funny or immature. She remains undecided.

In hindsight, our dating history seems kind of condensed. The day after graduation, we went on a date to Colorado, from New Jersey, in my Jeep, for four months. Years later, when our peers started clicking around Match.com and J-Date, our dates entailed climbing pyramids in Mexico and camping on the Napali Coast. By the time our peers began coupling up, we were honeymooning, in a canoe, in Zimbabwe. And when our peers started reproducing, we decided to wait—not because we didn't want to have kids, but because we did want to have mojitos at this bar in Cuba we'd read about, and the sanctions were supposed to be lifted any decade now. Ours was a relationship based on adventure; spontaneity; going out into the world. As a result, we skipped straight past the dating part and on to the long-term relationship part.

And now, I am about to tell you the two most important rules I have learned about long-term relationships, so you should pay attention because I am a guy who's been long-term relating for a very long term.

Dan's Rules of Long-Term Relationships

Rule 1: Happy, long-term couples can achieve a level of intimacy where words are no longer necessary; when their journey no longer requires a passport; when decades spent chasing down adventure pale in comparison to one quiet night curled up on the couch.

Rule 2: There's a fine line between a happy, long-term couple curled up on the couch and two carcasses who've fallen asleep to the same Netflix movie they've been trying to watch for six Saturday nights in a row.*

II.

"Would you like sparkling water or tap?"

This is the phrase that springs to mind when I think back to my last date with Megan. Loosely translated from English, it means: "Would you like sparkling water or tap?" It is a well-known phrase among couples like us who engage in a practice called date night.

Here's what date night is: date night is when you try to recapture in two to four hours, weekly or monthly, the kind of couple you used to be before you had to schedule something as goofy and contrived as date night. During this allotted time, the goal is to stay awake in each other's presence. Also to be nice to each other. That's why you have to do it off-premises, far from the distractions at home. Specifically, the distractions at home who are with a babysitter you found on craigslist for fifteen dollars an hour.

Revolutionary Road

We were skittish at first, so we didn't go far. Making reservations was out of the question since we never knew when we'd get out of the house. The babysitter would arrive around seven, and we'd spend the first fifteen dollars of her hourly rate tending to the children's shrieking separation anxiety. On a good night, we'd have them silenced by the thirty-dollar mark, at which point we'd bolt out and eat an egg roll around the block. We'd return at forty-five bucks, because that's when the sitter would call to say they were hysterical again. But this was in the early stages of date night, when we still believed those baby books that said it's bad to sneak out on your kids without saying good-bye because they'll get an abandonment complex. Now we never say good-bye. When the sitter shows up, we just turn on the Disney Channel and disappear. Our kids couldn't care less if we ever come back. It's a win-win.

Once we learned to abandon our children each Saturday night with no explanation, date night really blossomed. We still didn't go far, but we did cross the Brooklyn Bridge now and again to an island we once knew beyond the weekday hours of nine-to-five. In Manhattan, every night is date night, but on Saturdays, it's surprisingly easy to park. In a garage. For $25 an hour. We tried taking the subway a few times to save money, but there's no better way to kill a romantic night out than to sit next to a lady tweezing her chin on the F train. Except standing on a street corner for twenty minutes trying to flag down a cab. You get to a certain age when it's just easier to drive. In fifteen minutes, we could hop out of the minivan and into one of the many candlelit establishments Megan discovered in the "Tables for Two" column of her *New Yorker* magazine. Sure, date night looked indulgent once the AmEx bill rolled in at the end of each month. But, after all, this was New York. If we weren't willing to shell out our savings to enjoy it, then why stay in Brooklyn?

This question had been coming up a lot lately.

For me, it wasn't the cuisine I was willing to pay a premium for, it was the quiet. Date night was a chance to reconnect with my wife. There was no threat of spilled soymilk or stray Nerf bullets. There was just my beloved, and those deep green eyes I first fell in love with decades before.

"Do you think Leo has pinworm?" I would whisper into her ear.

"Come on, Dan. We promised not to spend another date night talking about the kids."

"Did you read that op-ed piece about the chlorofluorocarbons?"

"No, Josie spilled soymilk on it."

"Do you think Josie has delayed motor skills?"

III.

Somewhere down the line, we started dating other people. These things happen. We'd meet great couples all the time at school drop-off and pickup, but we'd never get to know them beyond the library steering committee or the Parents vs. Kids kickball game. There was this French couple we'd run into all the time in the family swim lane at the Y. There we'd be, barely dressed, torn between making small talk and making sure our kids didn't drown. These encounters were pleasurable, but ultimately meaningless. And so it was that date night begat double-date night. By going out with couples we found interesting, our thinking went, *we* would again be interesting. It wasn't romance we needed, it was co-mance.

For our first date, we asked out Max and Kim, who live in the town house next door. I made the first move. I was concerned that they were out of our league because Max and Kim are the kind of hip Brooklyn parents who still go out on week-nights. The couple of times I made advances, they said they already had plans. Then they followed up by suggesting a play-date for the kids the next day. To me, this was code for saying they just weren't that into us.

Imagine our delight when the couple they were supposed to go out with one Saturday night came down with swine flu. Flattered to be their understudy friends, we met at their favor-ite Ethiopian place on the Upper West Side, and engaged in spirited dinner conversation late into the night (9:00). As it turned out, Max *had* read the op-ed piece about the chloro-fluorocarbons. In his opinion, the real issue at stake was the global warming risk of the *hydro*chlorofluorocarbons, prompting me to weigh in with my concern about the spray-on sunscreen we've been using on the kids, which is that the reason we run out of spray so fast is because they make the cans really big but they intentionally don't fill them all the way up with sunscreen. Megan raised an interesting counterpoint with her belief that we run out of spray so fast because most of the sunscreen ends up getting sprayed into the wind instead of onto the kids. This was a compelling opinion, and one that led Kim to question why the spray-on sunscreen is freezing cold. Every time she sprays it on Shane, she noted, she's more wor-ried about frostbite than sunburn.

By dessert, we'd circled straight back to pinworm. Max firmly believed Leo didn't have it because if he did, he'd have a red rash on his inner rectum, like Shane did last year. Then the check came.

We dated Max and Kim on and off for a while, but the co-mance was too tied up in our kids. Now we're back to hosting playdates. It's just as well. As my mother always said (when she was talking about my father), there are plenty of other fish in the sea.

IV.

There are plenty of other fish in the sea, but not all of them are worth the cost of a babysitter. This is a lesson we've learned time after time in our quest for co-mance. But if you are among the companion couples who've accompanied us out on date night—and, frankly, after a few years on the circuit, I'd say the chances are good—promise you won't take it personally if things don't work out. It's not you, it's us. It's *all* of us. We chat each other up at soccer or ballet or Music for Aardvarks. We love our kids. We love them so much it aches. We love them even though we'd rather run our fingers across the serrated edge of a Saran Wrap box than explain to them calmly and respectfully to get in the goddamn bathtub. So, don't take this the wrong way, but . . . that's usually all we have in common. Maybe we have chemistry, but we rarely have history. You didn't know us back when we were those crazy college kids on the midnight train to Moscow, and we didn't know you when you were . . . whoever you were before we met you at the Dan Zanes show a few weeks ago (you know who you are). So we'll hook up for date night sometimes, and we'll all do our best to act like people instead of parents. I'll put on my special going-out slacks. Megan will use the thing to make her hair straight. We'll park a few blocks away so you don't see us get out of the minivan. First impressions count, right? We want you to understand the kind of couple we are, and the couple we used to be. *We* want to understand the kind of couple we are, and the kind of couple we used to be. But the four of us will get stuck at that awkward, getting-to-know-you stage. So we'll slip into that dispassionate, getting-to-know-you-through-your-kids stage. And from there, the writing will be on the wall. We never wanted to end it this way, but it's time to admit where all this is leading: to that heartbreaking, getting-to-know-you-through-the-rash-on-your-kid's-rectum stage.

V.

We first started having co-mantic feelings towards Claire and Justin when we started pre-K. I mean when Josie started pre-K. Claire and Justin's daughter was in her class. They were just our type. Justin was a freelance photographer, by which I mean a stay-at-home dad who stopped giving a shit after his darkroom was turned into a bathroom for his kids' playroom. His wife, Claire, was a successful advertising executive, meaning there would be another high-functioning adult for Megan to sit next to when date night rolled around. I courted them for more than a month before I finally wore them down. On our big night out, we went to an Italian restaurant near Coney Island. There, over a couple bottles of wine, a few appetizers, four salads, two antipastos, and five tiramisus (I was still hungry), the four of us got to know each other. Sparks flew. We connected. Their favorite character on *The Office* was also Meredith.

Only once did the conversation turn to lice shampoo.

"Hey, how did you guys first meet?" I interjected. A little abrupt, maybe, but I was doing my part to move them along to the "couple you used to be" conversation. As opposed to the "getting-to-know-you-through-the-parasites-embedded-in-your-kids-scalp" conversation.

It seemed they met on a subway car during rush hour. Claire was already seated when Justin got on, and he wound up standing over her.

"And he just locked my eyes," Claire said.

"Which is actually not like me at all," Justin said.

"And then he started flirting with me," Claire said.

"I was really, really attracted to her," Justin said.

"And I was totally *wet*," Claire said.

In the minivan on the way home, Megan and I conducted our customary postdate review.

"So that was weird," I remarked.

"What was weird? I thought they were great."

"The thing about her getting so turned on by Justin that she got *wet*? You didn't think that was a little too much information for our first date?"

"Oh my God, you are so sick," Megan said. "Her entire story was predicated on the fact that it had been pouring outside."

"Let's not start with the predicated. Just use normal words."

"Didn't you hear her say it was raining? She was soaking wet, but he still thought she was beautiful."

On some double date in the future, maybe I'll share this story with them and we'll look back and laugh. But it's too early in our relationship to tell if they'll think it's funny or offensive. I have to spend more time getting to know them. Next time I'll ask how their kid did with that lice shampoo.

VI.

Lately we've gotten involved with a younger couple. Our comance with Matt and Sharon has been electrifying. They're around fifteen years our junior. They're in the loop; they're up for anything; they don't have kids. It's that last quality Megan and I find most alluring. Call me delusional, but when we're with them, we don't have kids by association.

When we first started seeing each other, Matt worked at *Rolling Stone*, a publication that I myself wrote for prior to aging out of New Journalism and easing into Old Journalism. (Latest nauseatingly upbeat blog: "Why Getting Laid Off Is the Best Thing That Ever Happened to You!") A few date nights ago, Matt got us four free tickets for Fountains of Wayne. Sharon is a publicist, and she's always scoring tables at the hippest restaurants. I'm not talking white tablecloths and middle-aged parents choosing between sparkling or tap. I'm talking an urban farm shack in Bushwick called Roberta's, where the salad is grown in the parking lot and the crowd is composed of art school slackers drinking Brooklyn Lager. As always, the two of them brought us up to speed on music, art, and politics. And if we're robbing the cradle, well, call us a couple of crooks. All I know is they make us feel young again.

Except last time, which was when they made us feel old.

Matt got us on the guest list to this hidden hipster club called the Pharmacy. It had no sign and no phone number. The liquor was served from beakers, and the bartenders wore white lab coats. When Sharon ordered a beaker of ice water, it meant one of two things: Prozac or pregnant. I regret to report it was the latter. She was exactly one month in. We tried to act supportive as their conversation turned from designer drugs to lactation consultants, but our role had shifted to "mentor," and we've never been into that Svengali scene. I give the whole co-mance another eight months before we cool things off and try something new. Maybe we'll experiment with a same-sex relationship. But not Todd and Steven. The last time we did date night with them, neither one asked a single question about our kids. Not that we were offended. I mean, you know *us.* We're not the kind of couple who needs to talk about our kids all the time.

I shoved my new iPhone in front of Todd's face to show him a picture of Josie.

"It's gorgeous," he said.

"*It?*" I thought. *I think he just called my daughter "it."*

"Where did you get it?"

Where did I get it? I thought. *I got it from my wife's uterus.*

It finally dawned on me that he wasn't talking about Josie, he was talking about the swiveling, reclining leather chair on which she was seated.

I took back the phone and gazed at my perfect little princess.

"I got it from Crate and Barrel," I said.

VII.

Speaking of Crate and Barrel, Megan and I went out for our anniversary a few date nights ago. The evening began as we jabbed our way through the crowd at a formerly intimate French place we used to go to all the time before having kids. Finally, we made it to the maître' d, who cheerfully told us that the eight o'clock table I reserved would be ready in forty minutes. We weren't late. He hadn't given our table away. This is just how it works in New York. I no longer ask why.

We killed forty minutes by taking a walk around the neighborhood, a bustling stretch of SoHo filled with galleries and boutiques. And where should we wind up but at Crate and Barrel, which was having a 20 percent off sale on a king-size bed.

To recap: we spent our anniversary date night shopping for a king-size bed at Crate and Barrel.

If this was some kind of romantic comedy, the next scene would show me and Megan writhing around one of the beds in Crate and Barrel like a couple of college sweethearts on a midnight train to Moscow. But, instead, we strolled back to our 8:00/8:40 table for two. And as we sipped champagne cocktails, we came to an important understanding about our long-term relationship: There was no way a king-size bed was ever in a million years going to fit in our tiny Brooklyn bedroom. And that was okay. Because, after all these years together, we didn't need a king-size bed to make us feel comfortable. We didn't need expensive restaurants to make us feel sophisticated, or other couples to make us feel interesting. And, honestly, we didn't need anything as goofy and contrived as date night to make us feel like the kind of couple we used to be. We were soul mates. All we really needed after so many years was something very basic. A flat screen TV.

We watched *Fantastic Mr. Fox* on it last Saturday night with the kids. Best date night ever.

Some Friendly Advice to the Aloof Hipster Dad at the Playground

Hello there, Aloof Hipster Dad at the playground. I was hoping you might get off your smart phone for five minutes because, me and you, we need to have a man-to-man. I would also appreciate it if you could remove your ironically oversized Hugh Hefner sunglasses so we can maintain eye contact. Yes, also the big padded DJ headphones with the skull picture on them. I need you to go ahead and take those off for me. And the Bluetooth device. Thanks. Woops—do you mind not tweeting while we talk? I have a feeling I may be needing your undivided attention.

There is a question I would like to ask you, Aloof Hipster Dad at the playground. See that little three-year-old strapped into the black Bugaboo-brand stroller under the monkey bars, way over there on the other side of the playground? The little guy in the Sex Pistols T-shirt and the Velcro-strap Converse All Stars? Yeah, exactly—the one with the nose ring. Is that your kid? Pardon? For a second there, it sounded like you said, "I think so." Anyway, that kid has been crying his head off for fifteen minutes now, so I thought maybe you might want to go over and see if he's okay. Yes, I am sure it's not my kid who's crying. My kid is this individual standing next to us. She's actually the one who suggested we find you. She's four. How old are you? *Thirty*-four? Wow, I didn't realize they even *made* wallets with chains on them for thirty-four-year-olds! Come on, let's all go over there together. You ride your skateboard and I'll run interference if the nannies yell at you.

Look, we're here already! Did you notice how your kid stopped crying as soon as he saw you? That is because you are his father, and he was happy you came back! Don't mention it. Glad to lend a helping hand. And, by the way, there's just one more thing I wanted to tell you. Don't take this the wrong way, but, dude, you're making us look bad.

Yeah, *us*. Do you want to confirm what all these playground mommies and nannies have been suspecting about us all along? That we're morons? We've gotta show 'em we know what we're doing! We've gotta *organize*! We've gotta stop acting like a bunch of wusses and start acting like a team! Hey, are you a Giants fan? No? Then why are you wearing that Giants T-shirt? Oh, *They Might Be* Giants. Well, can we pretend it's a football jersey for a minute? Great, so pretend you're the player and I'm the coach. I'm going to draw you a diagram for your playbook. You got any sidewalk chalk? Of course you don't. Where would you put it? You don't even have cargo pants. But you know what? I'm gonna help you out with that, too. I'm gonna take you shopping for some cargo pants. I've got twenty-seven pairs of these things. Look at this: I've got the chalk in one pocket, the wipes in another, the juice box here, and the Band-Aids there. I look like a dork, but all of my shit is arranged. What's a juice box? I'm gonna pretend I didn't hear that. Okay, here's page 1 for our playbook:

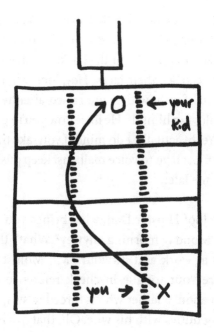

I hope I'm not coming on too strong, Aloof Hipster Dad at the playground, I really do. I'm just trying to help you out here. Trust me, the last thing I want to do is turn you into one of those Creepy Helicopter Dads at the playground. Look at that guy going down the slide with his ten-year-old over there. He's got his kid strapped to him with his belt. He's using his belt as a seat belt. Jesus. Promise me you'll have an intervention if you ever see me strapped to my kids on a slide. Promise? Thanks. See? We're already acting like a team. I do for you, you do for me.

And you know what I'd like you to do for me now? I'd like you to unbolt your kid from this giant black stroller here, and I'd like you to, you know . . . interact with him. I've got an idea. See that structure with the rubber seats that are hanging from chains? That device is called swings. Whaddaya say me and you push our kids on some swings? Come on, I'll show you how! I used to push from the back, but if you do it from the front, you can see their faces. Hey, look what the lips are doing on yours! See how they are raised at either side? That means he's enjoying himself. He likes how you're paying attention to him. Yeah, actually, I do mind if you take that call from your manager. Let it go to voice mail. Just keep pushing. You're gonna thank me later.

So, tell me, Aloof Hipster Dad, what brings you to the playground on a Monday morning anyway? What's that you say? Your wife is at work and it's your "Mr. Mom Day?" Good one! I admire your tongue-in-cheek reference to a thirty-year-old film about a father who is forced to swap stereotypical caretaking duties with his wife. Oh, that Michael Keaton. He sure was a moron! Remember that scene where he made his kid cook dinner and the kitchen went up in flames? And how he used far too much detergent to do their laundry? Ha, ha, ha.

Oh, you weren't saying it to be sarcastic? You were seriously describing yourself as Mr. Mom? Uh-oh, you're doing it again. Embarrassing us. If you're Mr. Mom, what do you think that makes your wife? Hey, mine's at work, too. But do you think either one of them walked in and said, "Good morning everyone, here we are for our Mrs. Dad Day!" So let's have a little dignity here. All we did was show up at the playground. That doesn't make us Mr. Moms. It makes us . . . I don't know what it makes us. It makes us dads. Not even. It just makes us parents. Parents with penises. PWPs. Say it loud, say it proud! No, don't really say it. Shhhh. I was kidding.

I'm beginning to like you, Aloof Hipster Dad. Though I appear dorky and you seem detached, I'm beginning to see that we're not that different. When it comes down to it, we're both a couple of dads trying to figure it out as we go. So you know what I'm going to do for you? Besides buying you the pants? I'm going to give you the benefit of the doubt. I'm going to assume that you don't really think you are too cool for drool. You're just in over your head like the rest of us. I've had more practice, that's all. You think I knew what to do back when my little girl here was a baby and she took a dump in the bathtub? No, actually, I didn't upload the clip on YouTube. I froze in revulsion. But then I learned. I learned to keep a soup ladle next to the bath toys. That's a tip I'm giving you right there. Ever had your head thrown up on? I have. Twice. Twice in the same day. A double-header. My son felt queasy on the flight to Disneyland so I put him on my shoulders when we got to the airport. Splat. Later that day, my daughter's too tired to walk anymore. Up on the shoulders she goes. Splat, splat. This is why I want you to wear a hat during family vacations. Yes, absolutely, that Mr. Bubble trucker cap you've got on will do just fine. Just turn it around so it's backwards like you used to do in the early '90s. You're gonna want the visor back there again. Added protection. Just remember who told you.

I can tell by the way you're tactfully trying to store your child back in your Bugaboo that you believe I'm done pontificating at you, Aloof Hipster Dad. Not so fast. They don't teach this stuff in school, you know. And we didn't learn it growing up, either. Back then, the role models were different. Things weren't the same when our dads were PWPs. I don't know about yours, but mine didn't know from cargo pants until they started selling them at Costco a couple years ago. So here we are at the playground—me, you, and that guy on the slide with the seat belt—making it up as we go. So let's step up to the plate already! Let's show a little hustle out here! Because I've got news for you, Aloof Hipster Dad. The mommies are losing patience.

You see them over there in the sandbox? Yeah, the "yummy mummies"; is that really what you call them? I wouldn't say that too loud if I were you. You piss off the mommies, you're gonna get hurt. They can beat us up, those mommies. They have anger issues. What do you mean, "with who?" With *us*! They talk about us all the time. I've been coming to this playground a few years longer than you have, my friend, and let me tell you, I've overheard it all. See that mommy with the pink pail and shovel? Right now she's complaining about how her husband let their kid play Cookie Doodle on his iPad for five hours on Saturday because he said it was raining out. And that mommy at the picnic table? She's bitching about how her husband has been laid off for three months, but he still asks her what's for dinner each night. And look at that mommy who's staring at us and trying to act like she's not. She's bad-mouthing some dad who had her kid over for a playdate a long time ago. When she came to pick him up, the kid was in front of a laptop with the guy's son, watching *Gilligan's Island* on Hulu. Between me and you, I didn't know what the big deal was. I was sitting right next to both of them the whole time, supervising the playdate.

How foolish I was. How much of a moron.

I have a theory about the mommies I would now like to share with you, Aloof Hipster Dad at the playground. I think they're trying to shut us out. On the one hand, they want us to be more involved, but on the other, they don't think we're up to the task. Why do you think they call all those classes "Mommy and Me"? You think they're trying to make us feel *comfortable*?

It's code: No morons allowed. So here's what we've gotta do. We've gotta get out there and show 'em we're man enough for Mommy and Me! You want to come with me to Mommy and Me swim class after this? Yes, I definitely think you'll still have enough time to take your kid to the gig your band is playing in Williamsburg later. What time does it start? Oh, midnight? Well, that certainly leaves plenty of time. Come on, what do you say? If you come, that'll make four dads in the pool. We'll represent! We'll make them call it Daddy and Me! Let's see how *they* like it.

Really? Your kid loves shooting pool? Hmm, I think you misunderstood, but that is pretty impressive for a three-year-old. What a terrific job you've done projecting your edgy hipster interests onto him! How about we just do a playdate? I know what you mean. To be perfectly honest with you, I still don't feel entirely comfortable saying that word, either. It's a goofy, goofy word. But I'll tell you something to make you feel better. It gets easier with practice. Come on, I'll say it with you. "Playdate." Now say it like a man. "Playdate!" Own it! Repeat it! "PLAYDATE!"

Fine, you wanna call it a hang, we'll call it a hang. So what do you want to do with these two for their hang this afternoon? Nope, I haven't been to that cool new bar in the basement of the Bed-Stuy housing projects. No kidding. Your kid loves the Pabst Blue Ribbon they serve in cans there. How did you find that out? Actually, don't answer that. Hey, maybe you and I could meet up for a beer sometime without the kids. We'll make a night of it. We'll go shopping for cargo pants first. But right now I was thinking more like the zoo. They have a camel you can ride with your kids near Congo Village. It's like a tandem camel. You gotta try this thing. Come on, we'll take my minivan. I get free parking. Why do you think I became a member? To protect animals? No way! Free parking! See how I'm kidding around? That's because I've grown so comfortable with you. So what do you say? Are you in?

No, sorry, I don't have any four-twenty. I actually don't know what you're asking me. Do you want to know what time they feed the sea lions?

Ah, that's a bummer that you can't make it. But I better be going before the line for that camel starts getting crazy.

I hope I run into you again sometime, Aloof Hipster Dad at the playground. But just in case, would you mind if I leave you with a little friendly advice? Next time you're lucky enough to have one of your "Mr. Mom" days, give it a try without your giant padded headphones and ironically oversize Hugh Hefner sunglasses. Because, dude, you're missing it.

Directions for Enjoying Disneyland

W hen the kids were still babies, I was still gung-ho about showing them the world. "Once Leo learns to walk, we'll take him to Cairo to climb the Great Pyramid," I'd fantasize. "Okay, Josie's eating solids. Let's fly to Mumbai so she can try Chicken Vindaloo." The goal of family travel, I formerly believed, was to expand our children's cultural horizons. The goal of family travel, I currently believe, is to avoid stowing them in the overhead compartments until we have begun our final descent. They're cute, our kids, they've just proven to be less portable with each passing year.

I mention this stuff to let you know why my wife and I selected the exotic and educational land of Disney for our first family vacation. At the time, Leo was five and Josie was two. Disneyland's claim to be "the most magical place on Earth" was very compelling. If it was true, it meant our children would get through the week without killing each other. We never imagined depleting our frequent-flier miles so our kids could experience the birthplace of consumer branding, but I'll tell you what, we also never imagined letting them eat a bag of Pirate's Booty for breakfast. Guess what they had this morning.

Maybe you, too, are inching closer to that inevitable expedition to the Magic Kingdom. And maybe you are saying, "Dan, you are a man who has strapped on a pair of mouse ears and tackled the terrain of Extreme Theme Park Travel. Please, share with me your many secrets so that I may follow in your footsteps without becoming a danger to myself and others."

Or maybe not. In any case, you are merely one sentence away from:

Dan's Disneyland Dossier
(in convenient FAQ format)

(FAQ) What should I bring to Disneyland?

(A) The most important thing to bring is my younger brother, Richie, who is a licensed social worker specializing in early childhood development. Growing up, Richie was always the most patient Zevin. To this day, I have never seen him lose his temper. Sometimes I think he doesn't even have a temper. Then I remind myself that he just doesn't have kids. When he does, he will presumably find his temper. And when he brings his kids to Disneyland, he will presumably lose it. Until then, I cannot recommend him highly enough.

With Uncle Richie around, you won't waste your precious Disney days listening to everything your kids want, and telling them everything they can't have. Relinquish your parental duties to him, and you will watch in wonder as they walk straight past five (5) souvenir stores in a single afternoon. Uncle Richie has a master's degree. He is trained to reason with youngsters determined to have a claustrophobic episode on the *Finding Nemo* submarine ride, even when the back of the line stretches all the way to the border of Tomorrowland and Tijuana. Have you ever heard of "dramatic play"? Uncle Richie wrote his dissertation on it. He believes it is therapeutic for children to bounce up and down indefinitely while screaming "I'm Tigger; No, *I'm* Tigger!", even when they are bouncing on his bed, on his vacation, on his pelvis, at 6:30 a.m. Unlike his elder brother, Uncle Richie never uses time-outs as a threat. He doesn't even *say* "time-out." He says, "Take some space of your own," and he says it like they're about to get a prize instead of a punishment. "Leo," Uncle Richie says, "how about if you take some space of your own to think up something fun for us to do instead of flinging that chocolate volcano at your sister?"

(FAQ) What is a chocolate volcano?

(A) A chocolate volcano is what they serve you for dessert at the Rainforest Cafe, one of numerous theme restaurants we sampled during our stay in Disneyland. The theme of this particular venue was to scare the living shit out of our daughter.

There we all were, happily enjoying our nightly intake of chicken fingers, tenders, strips, and/or nuggets—this time surrounded by smiling stuffed elephants, fuzzy toy gorillas, and/or chirping tropical birds. Suddenly, the place goes pitch-black, a roar of thunder rips through the room, and a simulated lightning storm sends the taxidermy into a frenzy of shrieking and squawking.

Once the lights came back, we were grateful to be dining with a pediatric social worker who could provide early intervention for Josie's future post-traumatic stress disorder. Uncle Richie classified her as "totally freaked out." He prescribed the chocolate volcano as a short-term remedy. Little did he know this remedy would be dispensed by a team of actor/waiters who stampede around your table screaming, "Vol-can-o! Vol-can-o! Vol-can-o!"

Note: Prior to procreating, Megan and I backpacked through our share of rain forests (as opposed to rain forest cafés) and once, in Indonesia, we even saw a real (as opposed to chocolate) volcano erupt. It was pretty scary.

The presentation of the chocolate one was scarier. I finally had to slip one of the screaming actor/waiters ten bucks and ask him to take it down a notch. By that point, Josie was so inconsolable that Megan had to rush her back to the hotel room with Uncle Richie. Leo and I stayed behind to pay the bill. And eat the volcano. Which, speaking as your travel adviser, I would describe as the single most outstanding food I have ever tasted. Even better than the chocolate-covered frozen banana with peanuts on a stick that Leo and I shared in Tarzan's tree house earlier that day. And, believe me, I'm a guy who's serious about his dessert.

(FAQ) Like all normal parents, we've instilled in our children a deep love of Mickey and the gang. Now that we're finally taking them to Disney, how can we make sure they'll come face-to-face with all their favorite characters?
(A) It brings me shame to confess that my wife and I did not provide our children with a solid early foundation in the characters. "We're going to Disneyland!" we announced a couple of weeks before we left. "You'll get to meet Donald Duck! And Goofy! And, you know . . . that other dog!" They stared back blankly, like we just said we're taking them to Slovakia to meet Ivan Gasparovic.

And thus commenced our pre-Disney indoctrination program. It was encouraging that Josie at least recognized Minnie Mouse and Winnie-the-Pooh. This was only because Minnie was on her diapers and Winnie was on her potty seat. She called him Winnie-the-Poop. I never corrected her in the past because I thought it was funny how she associated the cuddly critter with excretory functions. But now the time had come. The time had also come for Megan to sit her down for a mother-daughter heart-to-heart about Snow White and the Seven Dwarfs, and for Grandma Linda to present her with a preparatory pair of Cinderella slippers. Meanwhile, Leo and I spent intensive indoor time studying www.Toontown.com and immersing ourselves in *Peter Pan* (two-disc platinum edition).

It was clear that our crash course paid off from the moment we checked into our hotel. There, smack in the center of the lobby, stood a towering plastic statue of a certain silly dog wearing a yellow hat and floppy shoes.

"Goofy! Goofy!" Leo hollered, sprinting laps around it in a gratifying display of character retention. Josie froze, awestruck, and beheld the statue of Goofy the way an art scholar might behold the statue of David. Something went surging through her two-and-a-half-year-old veins in that moment; something like the first rush of estrogen. Slowly, she approached Goofy Statue and embraced it, tenderly. She then placed her hand in Goofy Statue's hand, the very one with the white glove. Fifteen minutes later, Josie and Goofy Statue were still hand-in-hand. It was heartbreaking, but she had to hear the truth.

"That is not *real* Goofy," I whispered to my little girl. "But I promise you this: By the end of the week, I will find him for you."

(FAQ) So? Did you find him?

(A) It wasn't easy, I'll tell you that. I don't know about you, but, back in my day, Goofy and the gang were just everyday people—or everyday whatever they are—who walked around giving high fives and riding the monorail like the rest of us. But when I returned with my own kids, they were all of a sudden these fancy stars who didn't go out in public.

Real Goofy was not to be found hanging out in Frontierland. He was not to be found in Adventure-, Fantasy-, nor Tomorrowland either, and he was definitely not to be found at Mickey's House, which I thought would be a sure thing since the two of them always seemed pretty tight to me. After thirty-five minutes of waiting on line inside, we were finally admitted into Mickey's private "movie studio." Can you believe he has a movie studio? In his *house*? This is where the now reclusive rodent receives his fans for a ninety-second photo op. We purchased our autographed 8-by-10 glossy and were promptly escorted out through the back door.

(FAQ) Whoa, that is harsh. When did the Disney characters go all Hollywood on us?
(A) Mickey turned into an asshole the day he got his own video game. As for the rest of them, my professional opinion is that the ABC merger went to their heads. Either that or they're afraid of stalkers. Whatever it is, just listen to me: If you want access, you go to them, they don't come to you.

(FAQ) Why didn't you just listen to your wife and do Breakfast with the Characters like she kept suggesting all week?
(A) Because I'm incapable of interpersonal communication at least until lunch. But when Megan finally pointed out that the characters are mute, it sounded much more doable. Josie would get to meet Real Goofy, and we would get a JPEG to e-mail the grandparents.
My wish (I mean, Josie's wish) came true by the build-your-own waffle station. There, Real Goofy was hobnobbing with a couple of characters I didn't recognize. I overheard some kid say they were Lilo and Stitch, but as far as I was concerned, they were just in the way. I especially didn't want Lilo in my

JPEG. Have you ever seen her in person? Let's just say she's not very photogenic. I mean, yeah, it's great for little girls to learn they don't all have to look like Sleeping Beauty, but this Lilo really looked like something was wrong with her. Like a hare-lip or something. But what do I know? It was morning. Maybe she just hadn't put her makeup on yet. I'm sure she has a great personality. She was very nice when I asked her to get out of the way so Josie could pose with Real Goofy. And the waffles weren't half bad either. All in all, a nice way to end the week.

(FAQ) Will you be returning to Disneyland for your next family excursion?
(A) No.

(FAQ) Why not?
(A) Because our kids are getting older. By this time next year, we'll finally be ready to take them somewhere to expand their cultural horizons.

(FAQ) Where?
(A) Legoland.

Semi Guitar Hero

As the sun goes down on a warm Wednesday night, a group of us has gathered in a cozy children's shop, surrounded by toddler-size cowboy boots, stuffed chimpanzees, and Melissa & Doug puzzles we feel good about because they were not made in China. After three weeks, we know nothing about each other, but that's cool with us. Here, it doesn't matter if we're attorneys or traders or writers of nauseatingly upbeat blogs. Here, we check our identities at the door, next to a rack of "Made in Brooklyn" onesies. We are here, at The Bubble Garden, for one reason and one reason only: to *rock*.

"So how'd it go with 'Wheels on the Bus?'" asks our teacher, Ally, a sweet, Suzanne Vega–looking blonde with the supportive disposition of a life coach. Ally is only slightly larger than her guitar, but her frame of reference is formidable. I have held her in high esteem from the moment she first compared "Itsy Bitsy Spider" to Nirvana's "Come As You Are."

"Did everyone get a chance to practice?" she asks. "Did *anyone* get a chance to practice?"

Ally hears the groans, but Ally does not judge. She knows that no one here plans on headlining Lollapalooza. We just want to learn a few old-school classics. And in seconds, our guitar picks are flying. We're completely off-key. Our timing is terrible. We. Are. *Rocking!*

"The babies on the bus say wah-wah-wah, wah-wah-wah . . ."

I can't believe I almost deleted her e-mail. At first, it looked like spam from yet another trendy kid's store that had conveniently forgotten to include an Unsubscribe button along with their weekly updates of Toddler Pilates and Physics for Infants classes. In this one, students could learn how to play children's songs on a guitar. But it was aimed at parents, not kids. And not just any parents, either, but parents like me— "Parents Who *Rock!*"

That's what the course was called, anyway, demonstrating that Ally was not only a Juilliard-trained instrumentalist, as her bio noted, but also a savvy businesswoman skilled at the marketing strategy known as "wish-fulfillment." A more realistic description would have been "Parents who *want* to rock," or "Parents who don't have *time* to rock," or "Parents who definitely do not rock but want to learn guitar so his kids will think he's awesome." And if not awesome, then maybe they'd feel slightly less apathy toward him. Because, let's face it, every little kid wants his or her parents to be proud of them, but nobody ever admits the reverse is true, too. But what did my kids ever see me doing that they could possibly be proud of? Staring at my laptop? "Hey, Dad, high-five on using italics to stress your point!" Tearing downcourt to dunk the winning shot? Just a pie-in-the-sky dream after injuring my knee (and before injuring my knee). Separating the recycling? Yes, they spend a great deal of time watching me separate the recycling. Not to mention dragging it out to the curb. Though they didn't see me getting a ticket from the department of sanitation for putting a lightbulb in with the glass, which evidently isn't allowed. But they probably heard me using some colorful language upon noting the $50 fee.

Anyway, it was time I had a hobby. The closest I've ever come was collecting Wacky Packs, and that was all downhill once I got Cap'n Crud. All these years later, the choices were limited. Choosing a hobby is tricky when you're a parent. You need to find that guilt-free blend of something you're doing both *for* your kids and *without* your kids. Learning guitar seemed ideal. In the best-case scenario, they would follow in my footsteps.

Let me clarify that. They would follow in *my* footsteps, rather than the footsteps of a certain, more famous father they'd been following in since they could walk. Every Halloween, he'd strap on his guitar and lead the parade at Cobble Hill Park. As a parent who *really* rocked, this guy was Brooklyn's Pied Piper. He wore a tall, slightly crooked Dr. Seuss hat and skintight striped jeans, and when he marched through the crowd playing "All Around the Kitchen (Cock-a-doodle-doodle-do)," the neighborhood kids went nuts. One year, he knelt down and let my son touch his guitar. I've never seen Leo look at anyone so worshipfully. Especially me. Not even on recycling night. And I haven't even mentioned how hot the mommies all get for this daddy. You know what they think when they see him? *DILF.* If it weren't for the police presence, they'd be rushing the stage and throwing their nursing bras up at him.

Not that I'm jealous. Why, do I sound jealous? Why would I be jealous? I think it's *great* that this guy is a gifted musician who was a real rock star before he became a kid's rock star. I *respect* his choice not to pack it in and stop giving a shit like various other individuals in his age bracket. I *admire* the humongous house he lives in that is ten minutes away from mine, on the nicest street, in the best school district. And, finally, I am *flattered* whenever people point out that I sort of resemble this much more famous father. It happened most recently when an attractive group of mommies came charging at me with their jogging-strollers one day and remarked: "Oh. We thought you were someone else."

Observe:

Photo A: Dan Zanes   **Photo B: Dan Zevin**

Upon studying the Dans depicted above, it may appear that the primary difference is four simple letters. That is incorrect. The primary difference is that the children who live with the Dan on the right think the Dan on the left is way more awesome.

"Okay! Let's move on to 'Old MacDonald Had a Farm'!"

Heading into the midterm stretch, attendance at guitar class had dwindled down to four parents who rock. There was me, the guy in the blue business suit who always sat next to me, the pregnant lady, and Carl from Brooklyn Heights. But really there were only two parents who rocked, since the pregnant lady wasn't due for like a month, and Carl, confidentially, just didn't rock. He was so uptight. One night, we were all jamming out on "Old MacDonald Had a Farm." Ask any parent who rocks, and they'll tell you there's a tricky lick in that tune where you have to make your fingers go from G to C. Basically, the idea is to get your hand into the gnarled position of a person with rheumatoid arthritis. It's frustrating. But it's especially frustrating the first time you finally manage to do it, and so does everyone else, and suddenly everyone is playing the same chords at the same time, like real rock stars, like Dan Zanes, and for a split second, you stop thinking about the position of your fingers and start grooving on the message of the song.

And on that farm he had a—

"Um, pardon me?"

Carl again, shooting his hand up and waving his guitar pick.

"I apologize, but is anyone else having a problem reading the tablature? It's probably just my vision but you've obviously all noticed me hitting the wrong frets and, Ally, I guess I should really be asking *you*, what exactly am I doing wrong or is it . . . Oh jeez, you all must think I'm such a dweeb for slowing everything down like this, so . . . okay, I'm just going to . . . okay."

I felt sorry for him the first couple of classes, but his self-consciousness started harshing my buzz. Who cared what anyone else thought? Learning something new this late in life was a chance to let it all hang out. It would be different if we were trying to learn an instrument in our awkward adolescent years, like normal people do. But we weren't normal people. We were parents. And if we ever expected to break out to that next level of being Parents Who *Rock*, the first step was being able to relax.

I didn't have a big issue relaxing. By the time class started at 7 each Wednesday night, I'd have a glass of wine or two in me from dinner. My family ate fast on Wednesdays, enabling me to ditch them at home and dart off to class. Once a week, for eight weeks, for forty-five minutes, I was a solo act. No kids. No spouse. No dog. To the untrained eye, I was just some funky rocker dude walking down Atlantic Avenue with a guitar strapped to his back, off to his gig at the Bowery Ballroom. Assuming the Bowery Ballroom still exists and isn't a Bank of America yet.

Occasionally, I'd run into someone I knew. "Wow, I didn't realize you played," they'd say, mentally recalibrating my Brooklyn Hipster Quotient (to 0.1). When they asked what kind of music I played, I described my style as "mainly Mother Goosey stuff." I could almost hear their hipster meters crashing back down. So I became more open-ended. I said I played "covers" and we left it at that. Then I'd continue walking down Atlantic Avenue like some funky rocker dude with a guitar strapped on his back, off to his gig at the Bubble Garden.

I have to get back to this guitar backpack for a second. If you yourself have never experienced the boost in self-esteem that comes from wearing a guitar on your back after years of wearing a Gerry TrailTech Backpack Baby Carrier that you got on craigslist for eleven bucks, I urge you to get yourself to Guitar Center at once. You don't even have to buy a guitar. Just buy the backpack. Then walk proudly about your neighborhood with your gig bag (you should definitely call it that), and you'll see what I'm talking about. There will be a spring in your step. The clouds will part and the sun will shine. Your friends will be impressed that you were at Guitar Center while they were at The Home Depot.

And don't listen to my friend Doug if he tells you the salespeople will blow you off unless you're Eric Clapton. That's what he told me, too, and it wasn't true. Maybe it was true back when Doug bought *his* first guitar (at the normal age of thirteen). Or maybe the salespeople actually thought I was Eric Clapton. I doubt it, though. They probably thought I was Dan Zanes. Unlike my children, however, they didn't seem disappointed to find out I'm not.

As soon as I walked in, three skinny sales guys with rock 'n' roll sideburns were all over me, treating me not like some dorky dad here to purchase his midlife-crisis guitar, but like one of them. In the background, Arcade Fire blasted from stadium-sized speakers. I don't know if it was really Arcade Fire. I have no idea what they sound like. I'm just assuming. That's how cool this place was. It was like stepping back in time to a pre-parental era when music mattered; when I drove five hours to see Pearl Jam play at the Orpheum Theater in Boston instead of tuning in to the twenty-four-hour Pearl Jam radio station on the Sirius XM satellite package that came with my minivan. As life got louder, I became drawn to the Ambient section of iTunes. Want to know the last thing I downloaded? Tibetan choir chants. I first heard it when I was trying to make reservations for date night at a restaurant in the city. The hostess put me on hold, and it was playing in the background. I found it very soothing. Now I listen to it every morning before the kids come down for breakfast.

But at Guitar Center, music was still there to stimulate instead of sedate. I found myself racing around in a delirium, making a mental checklist of everything I didn't realize I needed at first. Four-thousand-dollar electric Fender Stratocaster. Check. Twin reverb combo amp. Check. American DJ Dyno-Fog professional fog machine. Check.

I left with the backpack and a store-brand acoustic guitar. I chose it not because it was cheap, but because it was cheap and *black*. Black seemed like a kick-ass color for a parent who rocked. I bet that's what Johnny Cash thought when he bought his.

Toward the end of our eight-week session, Ally asked us to come in with one special song we wanted to learn for our children. My first choice was "Rock N' Roll Dream" by AC/DC. I changed my mind when I found out it had the F chord, which I'd dispensed with at week one-and-a-half. The A chord and E chord I could live with. The C chord came in time. But I could not condone the F. The F came to stand for *frustration*, and *fear*. If I were to draw you one of the how-to diagrams Ally drew for us each week, this is what it would look like:

Dan's Guide to Guitar Chords

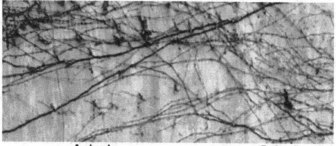

A chord   E chord

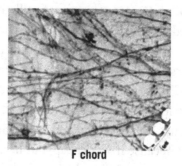

F chord

In class, whenever we performed anything in our repertoire involving F—"Twinkle, Twinkle Little Star" is one bitch of a composition that comes immediately to mind—I'd smile and air-guitar right over it. Like a high-functioning illiterate, air-guitaring was one of the sneaky coping mechanisms I used to hide my handicap. The other was air-singing. I mainly reserved that one for endurance rounds of "Row, Row, Row Your Boat," which always got a little demoralizing by the seventieth or eightieth round. And as long as I'm coming clean here, it didn't even occur to me to learn B^7, even when Ally said it would get easier once I got calluses on my fingers. I presumed she meant the three extra fingers I'd need to grow before I could possibly learn this cockamamie chord. Or maybe she just meant it would come with practice, which it didn't, since I also stopped practicing. It was hard enough to find fifteen minutes a day to master A, C, and E. Finding sixteen minutes or more to learn everything else was impossible. What began with B^7 would end with my estimated income taxes. A quick shot at switching from G to D would lead to the Y, where I was supposed to be taking the kids to their swimming class. No wonder the pregnant lady was shredding like Joan Jett by week number two. She didn't have any kids. But she would soon, and she'd find that when it comes to learning something new, there is a finite amount of time and brain space available to any parent, even one who rocks. I had learned three chords, and three chords was enough. It worked for the Ramones.

Excitement was in the air the night I gathered my family around for my highly anticipated, world-premiere performance of *"The Lion Sleeps Tonight."* I picked it as my special song because the whole thing consisted of A, C, and E (at least in the remedial diagram Ally gave me). On top of that, my kids loved that song ever since they heard the warthog and the ferret singing it with Simba in *The Lion King*. They'd seen me practicing for several weeks now, and if not several weeks, than at least several days, and if not several days, then at least that time they asked me to practice someplace besides the living room because they were trying to watch the Dan Zanes DVD. (Yes, he also has DVDs.) But now the moment had come. They were about to experience a seminal turning point in their childhood: the night they realized their dad was a rock star.

In the jungle . . .

"All together now!" I exclaimed.

The mighty jungle . . .

"One more time!"

I wrapped up with a Hendrix-style guitar solo inspired by "Purple Haze," except just in A, C, and E. I didn't take offense when our dog got up from the carpet and literally walked out on my act. Or when my wife broke into one of her giggling fits that start out cute but then turn a little creepy when she can't stop. The kids loved every minute, and that's all that mattered. Papa made them proud.

When the applause died down, Leo turned to me and said, "You forgot the uh-weeb-oh-wep part."

"My knee itches," added Josie.

Since the beginning of time, man has had wishes that have gone unfulfilled. The wish to fly, to attain eternal youth, to make your children think you're as awesome as Dan Zanes. And yet, we must persevere. Do I have any regrets about those eight wild weeks I took Parents Who Rock class? No is the answer. Except for one. I should have bought that fog machine. That would have completely blown them away.

The Long Limp Home

Show me someone who thinks "you can't go home again," and I'll show you someone who's never had surgery on their anterior cruciate ligament. I know what I am talking about here. I trashed my ACL on a ski slope in Vermont, and it led me on a post-operative odyssey to the house where I grew up in New Jersey. It was there that I spent a long weekend recuperating from my operation, and there that I experienced the single most prolific period of my life in letters. It happened like this. My surgeon gave me a prescription for painkillers. He also gave me a blank journal. It was entitled, quite eloquently, I thought, *Lower Extremity Rehabilitation Journal*. Filling out this journal was supposed to help me stick with the grueling physical therapy program I faced for the next three months. I cranked the whole journal out in the first three days. Except it wasn't the sort of journal he had in mind.

Now that my lower extremity is rehabilitated, at last my story can be told. It is presented here in its entirety, never before read by anyone, especially my orthopedic surgeon.

Dan Zevin

Dear Lower Extremity Rehabilitation Journal,

As I write these words, I'm lying in the bottom bunk of my childhood bedroom, staring at an autographed poster of Curly from the Harlem Globetrotters. I was discharged from the hospital two hours ago, and I'm relieved to be recovering here, among the manicured lawns and citizens of Short Hills. As I'd hoped, this is an ideal facility for assisted living: a convalescent-friendly ranch-style home, unlike the Town House of Scary Stairs awaiting me back in Brooklyn. Plus, it comes fully staffed with my father, Dr. Ronald, and my stepmother, Nurse Bebe. It is comforting to return to my suburban roots. My black vinyl beanbag chair still slouches on my orange shag rug, and my bookshelf still boasts the blue lava lamp I'd gaze at for hours, consumed by that innocent childhood dream to crack open the glass and examine the contents.

So here I am again, Lower Extremity Rehabilitation Journal, back in the house where I learned to walk. Only now, my leg is being strangle-held by a full-length metal brace that must remain locked day and night. I popped the first Percocet a half hour ago, but it still feels like a wrecking ball is smashing into my knee. Now where did I put those pills again?

Dear Lower Extremity Rehabilitation Journal,

Dad and Bebe just came into my room with a cold glass of Metamucil and a fresh plate of prunes. As I lie helpless in my bunk bed, they cleared away their past offerings—the bowl of Kellogg's All-Bran; the cup of barley soup; the half-eaten, whole-grain, double-fiber wheat toast. Everything is served with a side dish of Costco Organic Milled Ground Golden Flax Seed, "for the symptoms of discomfort accompanying irregularity." Already, I am touched by their eagerness to help me—specifically, to help me produce a bowel movement (as Dad puts it).

Here's the thing: I insisted on general anesthesia. On the plus side, I was nice and catatonic throughout my knee surgery. I was warned that constipation was a side effect, but it sounded like a win-win. If I was going to be immobilized for a few days, at least this would save me some trips to the bathroom.

I'm still adjusting to all this attention. I don't mean the attention to my bowels. Generations of Zevins have been attentive to the comings and goings of the family bowels. I mean the attention to *me*. I've gone from caretaker to caretaken; from the man of the house to the middle-aged boomerang kid. Meanwhile, my own kids are at home with Megan, whom I left to do everything by herself for the next three days while I lie here in my bunk bed shirking all responsibility. The guilt; oh, the guilt.

It's all so strange, trusty Extremity Journal. I've barely been away from the kids since they were born, and now it feels like something is missing. But what, exactly? The deafening noise? The relentless motion? Yes. Both of those. Here in Short Thrills, very little moves, especially me. Here, each day unfolds in the same sequence of soundproof, suburban seclusion. I will be served three fiber-rich meals per day; I will perform my range-of-motion exercises; I will adhere to a rigorous regimen of naps. The life of an invalid is challenging, but I refuse to spend my time here focusing on the pain. Instead, I will bravely focus on the vacation.

Dan Zevin

Dear Lower Extremity Rehabilitation Journal,

Did I just say vacation? I meant rehabilitation.

Dear Lower Extremity Rehabilitation Journal,

I took to my bunk bed at 8 p.m. tonight, hoping for peaceful, Percocet-assisted sleep. My plan was foiled by Dad doing karaoke again. Of all the birthday gifts I could have given him for his seventieth, why that freaking karaoke contraption? Oh, yeah. He asked for it. After a long and distinguished career in the field of obstetrics and gynecology, he'd expressed a sudden new interest in singing lead vocals. Who is to say, really, what inspires the artistic impulse?

Now that I think back, it all seemed to surface when he and Bebe drove to Brooklyn one weekend to see the kids. Josie was heavily into her Disney Princess Sing-Along Boombox. After her rendition of "Somewhere over the Rainbow," I saw Dad take the delicate pink microphone into his hands and blow on it, like a sound-check guy. Dad hummed something into the Princess Boombox that afternoon, but I can't remember what. Probably "Coming to America" by Neil Diamond. That was the number he led off with last year on his seventieth birthday, when I had the party for him at Sing-Sing Karaoke Club, this hipster hangout I saw reviewed in *New York* magazine. It was supposed to be a surprise, but the ones who seemed most surprised were the guys at a bachelor party in the back, especially when Dad's posse of seventy-somethings brought the house down with their grand finale, "That's What Friends Are For."

I think that's what he's singing right now, as a matter of fact. Nope. Sounds more like Barry Manilow, "I Write the Songs." Wait. Wrong again. I'm getting my crutches so I can go listen at the door. . . .

Cat Stevens. "Father and Son."

The label on the Percocet says "Take one to two tablets by mouth every four to six hours as needed." As needed. To me, that is a phrase open to interpretation.

Dear Lower Extremity Rehabilitation Journal,

It's 2 a.m. and I feel one of my spells coming on. It's been happening since I got here—these weird, vivid flashbacks to my youth. I guess it's not surprising considering that I'm here in my old bedroom. And considering that I'm completely disoriented. And considering that I spent a good chunk of my youth feeling completely disoriented here in my old bedroom.

It's 1973 and I'm in the backseat of Dad's Monte Carlo. He's driving me home from tennis lessons and listening to the same tape he's had in the eight-track player all spring. *Cat Stevens—Greatest Hits.* He's trying to talk about my serve. He trying to get me to follow through better. But mainly what he's doing is listening to *Cat Stevens—Greatest Hits.* He's becoming distracted by "Father and Son." "Father and Son" is getting louder in the backseat, and louder. Dad is becoming emotionally involved. Not rocking out, per se. Not drumming on the horn, or shaking his hair around. But concentrating. Concentrating on the *message* of "Father and Son." Then it happens. He turns around to face me at a stop sign, and I pull my terry-cloth headband over my eyes because I know. I know he's about to make one of his pronouncements and I know I'm just a kid and I know I'm not really going to grasp the crucial life lesson he is about to impart to me vis-à-vis "Father and Son" from *Cat Stevens—Greatest Hits.*

"Did you hear that line, Danny? *'You will still be here tomorrow, but your dreams may not.'"*

I finally get it, Lower Extremity Journal! I get Cat Stevens, and I get "Father and Son"! I didn't get it at the time—in fact, it made me want to puke at the time—but now, *I'm* a father, and back then, *my* father was a father, and actually he still is a father, and Cat Stevens was a father, and it's like . . . a whole cycle of fathers. And sons. And—*whoa.* I'm having a profound epiphany here. Everything is suddenly crystal clear, like a door has been unlocked. But why did it take until now to see it all so clearly? To what do I owe these mind-expanding revelations?

Dear Lower Extremity Rehabilitation Journal,

Note to self: Call CVS for Percocet refill.

Dear Lower Extremity Rehabilitation Journal,

Here's something that's starting to freak me out. My surgeon implanted "donor tissue" in my knee. *Donor* tissue. In other words, "dead guy" tissue. So: who was he? Or: who was *she*? Holy shit. What if I have a she-knee? What if I went in for knee surgery and came out a hermaphrodite?

Dear Lower Extremity Rehabilitation Journal,

I wonder what traits I'll inherit from her, this lady inside my knee. Hopefully, she knew some foreign languages. Or she had a knack for fixing small appliances like the dead Dustbuster I hid in the hallway closet at home after it got clogged with Cheerios. Fingers crossed.

One thing I already suspect is that she was good at crossword puzzles. My weakness in this area has always been a source of shame—until today at lunch (black bean burrito, bran muffin, lentil soup with flaxseed powder). Dad and Bebe were forty minutes into the one they always do together from the *Star-Ledger*. After all these years, they're still hardcore. They still use their special crossword puzzle dictionary. They still clock themselves with an egg timer. They still enjoy matching wits with *New York Times* Puzzlemaster Will Shortz, who does some kind of quiz show on NPR they've listened to every Sunday since I was a normal-kneed boy who lived here for real.

But here's the spooky part, L.E.R. Journal. When they asked if I knew an eighteen-letter word for "Fast Food Politico," I immediately blurted out, "Mayor McCheese." Not only that, I also got 23 down (kazoo) and 11 across (ointment) while they were busy washing my dishes. Okay, the more I write about it, the more I'm convinced. *I have the knee of a female crossword puzzle buff.* Maybe Will Shortz's mother. Mrs. Shortz. Assuming Mrs. Shortz is dead. And that she left her anterior cruciate ligament to science.

Wow, I just noticed that the rug in here is growing. Check out all the cool colors.

Dear Lower Extremity Rehabilitation Journal,

That's it, I'm quitting the Perc cold turkey. After reading that last entry, I'm worried about impaired brain activity. On the other hand, I'm also worried about withdrawal symptoms, specifically that wrecking ball sensation returning to my knee if I quit the Perc cold turkey.

Must do range-of-motion exercises. Must do range-of-motion exercises. *Hate* range-of-motion exercises. Especially hate range-of-motion exercise where good leg is used to bend bad leg back as far as it will go before screaming begins.

Must relax. Think happy thoughts.

Puppies . . . Rainbows . . . Painkillers.

Dear Lower Extremity Rehabilitation Journal,

Ah, what the hell. I can quit any time.

Dear Lower Extremity Rehabilitation Journal,

Time really flies when you're a controlled-substance addict. Already, it's day three of my recovery. Or is it week three?

It must be morning, for I hear the distant spray of Dad's Waterpik. I've noticed he's gotten extremely concerned with gum care. Not just his own gums, but the gums of his loved ones as well. Last night after dessert (oatmeal raisin flaxseed cookies), he presented me with a Waterpik to call my own. He got it at Costco, where he's spent a great deal of time since my arrival. I've decided that Costco taps into his Depression-era fear that, at any moment, he will no longer be able to provide his family with enough dental hygiene products. Or personal hygiene products, more importantly. The first thing I saw when I opened my eyes this morning was a fresh, white roll of toilet paper he left like an offering at my bedside. There was a note attached: "Good luck, Danny!"

Dear Lower Extremity Rehabilitation Journal,

No luck with bowel production, but I did have a rare opportunity to enjoy *Suburban Style* magazine in the quiet comfort of the guest bathroom. Megan called my cell as I was reading a how-to article on attracting hummingbirds to your backyard. As usual, she's been nothing but supportive. Every time she calls, she finds just the right thing to say.

"I know how hard it is on you, feeling so dependent on your father and Bebe," she'll say.

"Yes. You sure are correct about that," I'll say. "Having them do everything for me has been very, you know . . . *difficult* to adjust to."

"Just promise me you'll stay another day there if you need to. The kids and I can't wait to have you back in Brooklyn, but everything here is great, really."

But then some kind of curveball gets thrown into our daily chats. For example,

"EEE-OOO-EEE-OOO-EEE-OOO! HONK, HONK, HONK!"

"What's that horrible sound?!" I'll say.

"Oh, it's nothing, honey," she'll say. "Really, you have enough to worry about."

"Is that the car alarm? Are you in the minivan?"

"Yes, okay! It's been on for two days! Can you hold on a second? Josie, put your seat belt back on! Leo! For the last time, those DVDs are not Frisbees! Sorry, honey, gotta go. The tow truck is here."

Each time I finish these phone calls, I'm more certain we should be suburbanites. Once we leave the city, stress will evaporate. We wouldn't even need a car alarm. Our house would come with a garage. And one of those special rooms where you wipe your feet. What's it called? A mudroom! The children would have plenty of space to wipe mud from their sneakers after behaving perfectly in their private backyard, which would not contain a teenage truant sitting up in a basketball hoop, like that creepy cursing kid in the park by Josie's nursery school. And once we leave, we'll never turn back. Restaurants? I'm sure the dim sum is just as good at Applebee's. Diversity? Imagine all the different types of hummingbirds we'll attract!

I've got it all figured out, *Lower Extremity Rehabilitation Journal*. We'll live *here*, with Dr. Ronald and Nurse Bebe. They'll take care of *all* of us. It's brilliant!

Dear Lower Extremity Rehabilitation Journal,

I called Megan late tonight to announce our future life in Short Hills. Her reaction was that I was slurring my speech.

Dear Lower Extremity Rehabilitation Journal,

Leg lifts: 3
Quadricep extensions: 1
Sicko fantasies of remaining in bunk bed forever, wearing
giant flannel feet pajamas and leading life of deadbeat dad:
numerous.

Dear Lower Extremity Rehabilitation Journal,

Mom made a bedside visit today while Dad and Bebe were out
buying me better ice packs. She was on her way to Bed Bath &
Beyond to return an insufficiently scented aromatherapy candle. When I first saw her, I thought she was another Percocet
hallucination. After all, she hasn't been in this house since she
used to live here.

As always, pleasantries were exchanged.

Mom (inspecting foyer walls): Oh, wallpaper. When did
she have my paneling taken down?

Me: Thirty-five years ago.

Mom: Well, you gotta hand it to that Bebe. She certainly
doesn't waste any time.

Dear Lower Extremity Rehabilitation Journal,

Exciting news! Just produced a bowel movement! Not to brag,
but it was more like a bowel *removement*. As in, there's absolutely nothing left in there. Thank you, Kirkland Signature
Stool Softener with Bulk Forming Laxative Action. After three

days (weeks?), I am no longer blocked. I wish the same could be said for the toilet bowl.

Dear Lower Extremity Rehabilitation Journal,

Who else can a man trust but his own father to waterproof his braced leg with Hefty bags and duct tape, thoughtfully avoiding his son's sensitive personal region? That is what just occurred in preparation for the first shower I've taken in three days or weeks. Later today, I'll go home to my devoted wife and children back in Brooklyn. It seemed important that my knee brace and I look our best.

Maybe it was all meant to be, trusty Extremity Journal. The pampering, the coddling, the unprecedented attention to my personal well-being. The truth is that knee surgery wasn't such a setback after all. In the end, it gave me just what I'll need to return to real life. And I will take it by mouth every four to six hours as needed.

Tennis Menace

One day while pedalling a recumbent stationary bike and losing my will to live, I came across an article claiming that middle-aged men are the fastest growing demographic competing in triathlons these days. I nearly fell off. As a knee-surgery survivor for whom physical fitness had been replaced by physical therapy, I had a hard time accepting that this fast-growing demographic was anything more than the kind of nauseatingly upbeat bullshit I'd make up for my blog. Then I took a look around the gym, and there they were. Guys like me with the telltale signs of Male Pattern Oldness—receding hair, advancing guts, $300 padded headphones from the Hammacher Schlemmer catalog. The only difference was, they were the ones vigorously spinning, squatting, and triathlon training, while I was the one flatlining on the chaise lounge of exercise equipment. *What do they have that I don't have?* I asked myself about the fast-growing demographic. The short answer was: limbs that weren't fastened together with surgical screws. But the truth was that they had something more: the drive to recapture their youthful vim and vigor by proving they can still keep up with guys twenty years younger.

I don't have that drive very much. Of course I want to recapture my youthful vim and vigor (especially my vim), but it seems counterproductive to compare myself to guys twenty years younger. It works better for me to compare myself to guys twenty years older. Which explains, at least a little, how I turned to tennis.

Ever since I started rehabbing my knee, I'd been noticing these older, distinguished-looking gentlemen at my gym. They had white shorts, shirts, and hair. They held racquets instead of dumbbells. Breezing their way past the grunters doing leg presses, the groaners working delts, and the convalescent on his chaise lounge, they smiled instead of strained. I wanted in.

One day I followed them to an unmarked door in the corner that led them upstairs. *Upstairs*, where the high-altitude air quality was untainted by armpits and flatulence. *Upstairs*, where I would never again run into Chrissy, our newest date-night babysitter, or any of the post-college Zumba classmates she always brought by to meet me at the exact moment I was becoming drowsy on my recumbent bike. *Upstairs*, where endless green floor space and a trillion-foot ceiling was sealed in a bubble that looked like a cloud. Here, physical fitness was conducted by gentlemen, not Iron Men. Here, the civilized sport of tennis was being played.

My downstairs days were done. The youthful promise of getting ripped had become the middle-age reality of getting torn. Everyone I knew was transitioning from downhill to cross-country, running to jogging, basketball to softball to foosball. As for everyone else—i.e., the fast-growing demographic—I was pretty sure they'd be joining our transition team too, just as soon as they finished their triathlons and were released from the ICU. Eventually they'd reach the same conclusion I did that day: What goes on downstairs is a young man's game. But what goes on upstairs, as my father always said, was a game that can last a lifetime.

It had been a lifetime since I last played the game that lasts a lifetime, so I had some brushing up to do. Of the many technical skills I had to relearn, such as the forehand, the most challenging was the reserving of a court. There were only two up there. And it seemed like every time I asked the lady at the front desk, she said they were both reserved. I decided to seek advice from one of the kindly-looking gentlemen heading upstairs. Here is the first thing he said: "Well, it's nice to see the younger generation rediscovering the sport."

He introduced himself as Roy, and I liked him right away. According to Roy, whose judgment I trusted and respected, the trick was to call up the club on Thursday mornings at eight, because that's when they take reservations for the whole week.

I called Thursday morning at eight.

"Please hold."

I held.

"Can I help you?"

"Yes, I want to reserve a tennis court."

"I'm sorry, they're booked all week."

I told the lady that was impossible because I happened to know they started taking reservations at this time each week. My good friend Roy said so.

"Oh, you're a friend of *Roy*?" she said.

Finally I was getting somewhere.

"That's such a coincidence!" she continued. "He was just here reserving his court times while I had you on hold."

Long story short, Roy screwed me. Yes, he told me when to call the lady. No, he did not tell me that those who call are put on hold, while those who come in person are put on tennis courts. Somehow I expected more of Roy. Why, I don't know. I guess I fell for the old "younger generation" line. Or maybe I just forgot for a second that Brooklyn was becoming every bit as cutthroat as our sister city across the bridge. Oh, our bumper stickers all talk a good game about coexisting, but really what we're doing all day is competing. Competing for the parking space, the duplex, the nanny, the seat on the subway, the slot in the school, and—thank you, *Roy*—the last remaining forty-five minutes of court time. As the rare resident whose competitive streak had atrophied through the years along with his knee, I took what I could get: a spot on the waiting list in case someone cancelled. Amazingly, someone did, from 11 to 11:45 on Wednesday morning. The timing was perfect since it interfered with writing my latest blog for OldMan.com ("Triathlons: Easy As 1,2,3!!!").*

Once I reserved a court, it occurred to me that I required a person to play with. My main qualification was that he had to suck. This would ensure we'd be evenly matched. Also, he had to be free Wednesday morning from 11 to 11:45. Other than that, I just wanted to bang a few balls back and forth with someone who was in it for the camaraderie, not the competition; a partner, not an opponent. The first person I thought of was my former friend Larry because I remembered he also had something wrong with him, like fallen arches or a rotator cuff injury—wait, no, the rotator cuff was Paul; Larry was something else. Bursitis? Whatever, I can't remember. Larry and I ran in the same circles in our undergrad days at NYU. Now we mainly saw each other on Saturday mornings for Super Soccer Stars. This is what happens when friends become fathers. Going out with the boys means going out with the *boys*, or

*Please note nauseatingly upbeat usage of three consecutive exclamation points. Thank you.

going out with the girls if you have daughters. Anyway, I figured Larry would be free because, like me, he's a stay-at-home dad. Having human contact with someone who does not share our DNA is always a welcome change of pace.

Larry didn't suck at tennis, it turned out. But, as I'd learn on future Tuesday mornings from 11 to 11:45, he didn't suck in a very supportive way. "Nice lob!" Larry would say as I'd send another ball soaring into an overhead light fixture. "Good hustle!" he'd cheer if I managed to get it by the third bounce. We were playing our special version of no-impact, slow-motion tennis. But, I'll tell you, it felt great to be playing anything at all. Playing had become an activity reserved for the younger generation, the generation I spent schlepping around to playgrounds, playdates, and play spaces. As for my own leisure time, it seemed as if most of it was spent playing dead.

But, upstairs, I started coming back to life. Stabilized by my trusty Futuro brace, my knee felt better each week, and so did Larry's whatever he had (Sciatica? No, that was Mark. Cat scratch fever? No, that was my mother.). Before long, we progressed to playing actual games.

"Why don't you take a do-over on that one!" Larry would offer each time I double-faulted. "Great game!" he'd supportively say after killing me, 40–love.

"Thanks, man. I appreciate it," I'd respond, smiling and acting all sportsmanlike. Hey, I was in it for the camaraderie, not the competition. The last thing I wanted to be was a sore loser.

To prevent being a sore loser, I decided to find someone I could beat. It wasn't Lily's dad. I call him Lily's dad because that's actually how he shows up in my cell phone. I couldn't remember his name when he gave me his number at nursery school one afternoon, so I just typed in "Lily's dad." He saw my racquet poking out of my backpack, and said he'd be interested in playing. So I figured, what the hell, let me call Lily's dad.

Lily's dad was so happy to hear from me. He'd wanted to get back into tennis for a while, he said, because he thought it would be a good complement to all the training he'd been doing for his first triathlon. Lily's dad was disappointed to hear I was sick on the day we were supposed to play.

I miraculously recovered upon reaching my former friend Nate. I knew he'd be interested because he was a Realtor. Like all New York Realtors (and residents), Nate believes that any encounter at any time with any person or persons is God's way of providing a networking opportunity. Tennis was no exception. "Just name the time," Nate said. "You know what's funny? I'm doing an open house this weekend for a co-op in Park Slope. It has tennis courts on the roof! Come to think of it, you and Megan would *love* this place. . . ."

Playing with my former friend Nate was like playing with a coach. A coach who gave me tips. Loosen your wrist, tighten your grip, bend your knees, follow through, play the net, play the line, keep your eyes on the ball, try to stop thinking how much you hate me because I keep giving you these condescending tips. Oh, sorry, he didn't really say that last one. But I think you know what I'm getting at. The tips, they bugged me. They especially bugged me because they didn't work. The only point I ever scored was the time he double-faulted when I yelled, "Choke!"

I am being facetious, of course. I actually got another point later, when I said his shot was long even though it really wasn't.

Every now and then, I am reminded that I'm the luckiest man on planet Earth. Whenever I'm feeling blue about my backhand, troubled by my topspin, or down on my drop shot, I simply remind myself that I'm playing tennis while my wife is out earning a living. Some spouses might resent this arrangement, but not mine. She knows that tennis is *good* for our marriage, because it provides her husband with a way to burn off the energy he'd normally put into driving her insane. I wasn't as cranky on game days, Megan observed. She was right. I felt better. Since taking up tennis, I'd experienced a complete loss of the suicidal tendencies that surfaced as soon as I sat on that soul-crushing recumbent bike.

I still sucked, though. So Megan suggested taking lessons. I reminded her that I already took lessons. The lessons occurred during my sophomore year at Millburn High in New Jersey, a school with a zero-tolerance policy for any act that might be construed as noncompetitive. The unspoken motto of the Millburn athletics department was "You can't be in it if you can't win it." So I wasn't, because I couldn't. A late-to-never bloomer, the only growth spurt I had experienced at that juncture was my hair. Following a summer of intensive back-floating down the shore, it had broadened and filled out into a powerful, golden mop popularized at the time by Vitas Gerulaitis. Having Vitas Gerulaitis hair is what convinced me that tennis was my sport. For one thing, Vitas Gerulaitis seemed like the kind of guy who got laid a lot. (This didn't prove to be true for me, incidentally, especially when I started wearing his trademark wristbands.) For another thing, tennis was the one sport I was good at, by which I mean "less bad at," than every other sport, with the exclusion of pinball. Let me explain something to you about pinball. If the great game of pinball had been a varsity sport, I would have gotten into Princeton on a full athletic scholarship. Tragically, there was no pinball team at Millburn High. But there was a tennis team. And I was determined to make it. I took lessons at my dad's tennis club every single day for three, possibly two, days. Such was my drive to succeed.

For my fifteenth birthday, my mother got me exactly what I wanted: a new racquet. Actually, she got me two new racquets. The one that was exactly what I wanted was an aluminum Wilson T-2000. It was basically a handle attached to a Hula Hoop with nylon strings inside. She thought it looked too big for me, though, so she gave me a wimpy wooden Prince as a backup. She returned the Prince to the Short Hills Mall only seconds after I blew out the candles.

Having a racquet that was too big for me was the whole point. As I recall it, I was barely as tall as the net. But armed with my T-2000, a sporting good that even *sounded* like a weapon, there was no doubt that I would make the varsity team and spend the next several years fornicating with cheerleaders. All I needed now was that Millburn Varsity warm-up jacket; that satiny blue status statement with the two racquets crisscrossed on the back and my name stitched in script on the front. *Vitas Gerulaitis.*

Please allow me to steady myself before I tell you the next anecdote about my tennis team tryout.

Alright, I'm gonna make this fast.

You know those mechanical machines that hurl tennis balls across the net like torpedoes? I would like you now to envision twenty of those, except human, on one side of the net, and me on the other.

"Ready, aim, fire!" Coach Stalin shouted into his bullhorn.

And the next thing I knew, I was a writer.

A couple months after my first foray upstairs, I found myself back at the front desk, waiting for the clock to strike eight. You are correct in assuming I was first in line. My aim was to reserve a court around lunchtime for me and Max. I asked him to play because I'd recently observed him walking down Smith Street in those white Fred Perry tennis shoes with the green wreath logo on the side. In weeks to come, I would observe the majority of my neighborhood promenading around in the exact same footwear, not because they were into tennis, but because they were into sneaker worship, the predominant religious practice in Brooklyn.

A few minutes before the clock struck eight, I was struck with an urge to urinate. The guy behind me said he'd hold my place in line. I came right back, and he was gone. In his place, a white-haired gentleman by the name of *Roy* was feverishly filling out the sign-up sheet in his quest to reserve every slot that might fit into my schedule or the schedule of any actual or potential partners I might produce, commencing from this point on into perpetuity.

Me: What happened to the other guy?
Roy: He went upstairs to warm up before our game.
Me: Did he tell you he was saving my place?
Roy: Yes, but we had no way of knowing when you were
    coming back.

Playing at six o'clock in the morning on a Sunday was a lot more fun than it sounds, mainly because Max was hungover. To my great delight, he sucked more than I could ever have hoped. You should have seen me running him ragged in his ironic black warm-up suit and white Fred Perrys. I proudly wore a blue Adidas jacket in the vein of the varsity team, except my father got it at Costco. He also got me white tennis shorts, which I wasn't so sure about at first but then I decided they were okay because they showed off my lucky knee brace.

The truth is, I'd grown a little attached to my brace by this point in time. I thought it made me look sporty and athletic. I'm thinking of getting another one to put on my good knee, maybe in a different color. Or athletic tape. I'll wrap myself from head to toe, like a mummy, just to make sure everything stays aligned.

The one disturbing part about playing with Max was that he'd get really down on himself. A few times, he even yelled at himself in third person, like: "Jesus, Max! What is *wrong* with you?!" It was hard not to wonder what internal critic he was channeling. His father? Some lunatic Little League coach from his youth? To be honest with you, I didn't care. I was way too focused on how amazingly alpha it felt to be better at tennis than someone else. After a few volleys with Max, I developed the confidence to do the trick where you pick the ball up off the ground not by bending down like an amateur, but by dragging it to your ankle with the racquet and kicking it up with your foot. I call it the Ankle Hop-Up. It's my signature move. In weeks to come, I also started spinning my racquet around in my hand before Max served, another sure sign of a competitor. And guess which one of us shut the other one out when we played not just one but *five* games in a row, which, for those of you who are not as knowledgeable about the sport as I am, is what we call a "set." I mean six.

Yes, I had developed an appetite for the sweet taste of victory, but still I did not forget where I came from. Whether I was lobbing shots over Max's head or slamming them toward his testes, I gave him plenty of encouragement and pointers. "When the ball comes, you are supposed to hit it with your racquet!" I would encourage Max, or, "Okay! Now you can get up off the floor!"

I'm not kidding about that last pointer. Max tripped over

his Fred Perrys and sprained his ankle, leaving him in excruciating pain, and leaving me—more importantly—with no one whose butt I could kick on the court. Given time and physical therapy, his ankle would heal just like my knee did. But right now, his injury was a huge setback for me. A *sprained ankle*? A *sprained ankle* was going to end my winning streak? Excuse me. Have you ever heard of Millburn High? Listen, pal, nice guys finish last. If someone was going down on my court, I wanted him lying on his back and covered in blood. I wanted to plant my foot on his chest like a pro wrestler, and I wanted the line judge to hurl my arm up in victory.

"Who wants a piece of me now?!" I'd shout to the fans packed in to watch me at the U.S. Open. "Step up to the net, suckas!"

Do you believe in karma? Do you believe in What Was Meant to Be? I know, neither do I. But what if I told you now about one lonely week when I resigned myself to returning downstairs. There I was again, considering the various ways one could commit hari-kari on a recumbent bike, when a flyer by the water fountain caught my eye.

MASTERS LEAGUE FORMING.

Tennis players aged 40 and up wanted
for friendly, morning round robin.

I've left three messages so far, but the contact person listed at the bottom hasn't returned a single call. Way to go with the silent treatment, *Roy*. Oh, and Roy? I know where you're hiding. I'm comin' upstairs for you, Old Man River. There's a new Master in town. And he's packin' a T-2000.

A New Jersey Pilgrim's Progress

It wasn't until I attended my first New England Thanksgiving that I discovered cranberries are not a canned good. I was spending the holiday with my girlfriend's family near Boston, where the two of us had been happily living out of wedlock. Having grown up in a New Jersey household where Thanksgiving entailed a Butterball and a can of cranberry sauce (and maybe an extra-special side dish, like a defrosted brick of Bird's Eye string beans with built-in flavor flecks), I was ill prepared for the colossal significance New Englanders place upon the holiday they proudly claim as their own.

The members of her family took weeks to prepare a five-course fete. They did not dart up from the table, wildly waving a turkey leg, to see who was winning the Lions game. They even seemed to know what the hell it was that they were celebrating, which was very impressive to a Jersey boy whose primary knowledge of Plymouth Rock came from a cameo as Ear of Corn in a fourth-grade production of *Mayflower Power!* (To the best of my recollection, I had no speaking lines.)

Many years later, that girlfriend is my spouse, and the two of us hosted our own family Thanksgiving this year. We had long since moved to New York, but we couldn't have pulled it off without those formative turkey years we spent in New

England. I invite you to come along now as I turn back the clock, and share the secrets I discovered in the November of my youth.

How to Acquire the Main Course

First of all, you're not looking for a turkey. Turkey is something eaten in New Jersey. In the birthplace of Thanksgiving, I learned to look for "the Bird." It was a moniker of respect and status, not unlike the Queen, the Pope, or the Fonz. Anyone who acquired the Bird at a supermarket was considered a cheater (or from New Jersey). In Boston, the Bird was to be acquired at one of a select sampling of appropriate farms, preferably an outfit in Lexington called Wilson Farms, which was referred to by insiders (i.e., not by me) as simply "the Farms."

The first time I went in search of "the Bird" at "the Farms," I was really into it. It made me feel like one of those rugged New England guys, maybe one who actually grew up in Plymouth, who was only at the Farms in the first place because his annual wild turkey hunt was canceled due to fog. This romantic notion vanished as soon as I pulled into the second of the Farms' vast parking lots, only to find that it was harder to find a spot here than on trendy Newbury Street—from where, incidentally, it looked like many of my fellow Thanksgivers had just come. At one point, I was in line next to an extremely perfumed lady with the type of bosom that suggested silicone, and the type of strangely swollen features that suggested Botox.

"Are you *certain* that this Bird hasn't been injected with any chemicals or growth stimulants?" she was yelling at a terrified teenage employee. Ten minutes later, she cut me off in the produce aisle and swiped the last sweet potato. But, hey, at least she left with a Bird in her basket. I myself left empty-handed. Unbeknownst to me, you were supposed to reserve your Bird weeks in advance, as if you were trying to book a table at the Ritz-Carlton downtown.

On the drive back to my apartment in Somerville (then known as Slummerville), I stopped at a Star Market and bought a mere "turkey." I cheated. But I learned from the error of my ways.

Proper Bird Preparation

No one likes a dry Bird. Back in New Jersey, we simply accepted the fact that turkey is, on the scale of arid to damp foodstuffs, you know, on the dryish side. So we'd just pour our can of cranberry slime on it to moisten things up a little. If you want wet food, the thinking went, you wouldn't serve turkey. You'd serve soup.

In the home of Thanksgiving, however, your very dignity is at stake if you became associated with a dry Bird. You learn that a dry Bird is a sign of weakness. "If I serve a dry Bird," you believe, "I will be ostracized from the community and probably stoned to death."

Everyone in Boston seemed to have their own theory about the best way to prevent dry Bird. The year we got married, Megan and I were persuaded to try a meshuga technique called "brining," which entailed submerging the Bird in salt water for several days prior to cooking, presumably so it got waterlogged enough to stay moist even after spending the rest of the day in a Radar Range.

If I'm not mistaken (and I usually am), we discovered this procedure in *Cook's Illustrated*, the kind of fetish publication that publishes forty-seven-page think pieces on spatulas. It makes perfect sense that this magazine was published in Boston. It appeared to be produced by lots of individuals with PhDs.

I am not in possession of a PhD, which may explain why, after brining the Bird for forty-eight hours in a jumbo plastic pail normally reserved for mopping, my recollection of the Bird's texture is that it was: dry.

It took a few more New England Thanksgivings to learn that what you really need to do is baste, not brine. Baste, baste, baste. That is my advice. It is also my advice to stay away from those "self-basting" turkeys we used to get in New Jersey. Real New Englanders never went in for the self-basters. They *were* the self-basters! From their point of view, basting built not only character but also muscle. And you want to know something? They were right. You should have seen me this past November when Megan and I hosted Thanksgiving in Brooklyn. I power-lifted the whole hulking pan approximately every ten seconds, tilted it on its side, and maintained this position in an isometric fashion long enough for my wife to make sure everything got fully squirted. Maybe I'm not the rugged New England guy I once was, but I can still eat as much pumpkin pie as I please, thanks to the calorie-burning basting regime I've stuck with all these years. I am going to request that a Baste class be added to the roster of Spin and Zumba classes conducted downstairs at my health club.

Presenting the Bird to Others

Back in New Jersey, we never actually saw the whole cooked turkey prior to eating it. We heard it. We'd all be sitting in the dining room, yelling and interrupting each other (the standard Zevin mode of communication), when suddenly, from the kitchen, we'd be drowned out by the roar of a chain saw. It was, of course, my mother, revving up her trusty electric knife.

That first Thanksgiving in New England, I understood that poultry should be seen, not heard. My future mother-in-law glided from the kitchen with the most magnificent display of fowl I'd ever laid eyes on—a whole Bird big enough to obstruct the view of the guest across from me. It sat regally on a sterling platter, and a hush fell over the room. When I think about it today, I imagine it dressed in a wedding gown, with a tiara perched atop its . . . leg.

Then my future father-in-law swiftly ushered the Bird back into the kitchen, and set forth to carve it with the precision of a woodworker. I don't know exactly what went on back there, but, when he returned with our carvings, it was clear we were in the hands of a master. I still feel guilty for eating his work. I should have donated my portion to the Museum of Fine Arts.

"Would you like some cranberries with that?" I was asked. I scanned the table for a cylinder of Jell-O-like "sauce," but was handed a porcelain bowl of warm berries instead. No one was more excited than I to hear that they came from a bog on the Cape.

"How about some beans?" Green beans, white beans, kidney beans, garbanzo beans, Mexican jumping beans, for all I know—and not one was prepared in a microwave set on "defrost."

"Bread?" Unsliced. Brown, not white. Served with a personal side dish of olive oil, not a family-sized tub of I Can't Believe It's Not Butter. By desserts (half a dozen different pies that did not come in white boxes wrapped in string), I was plotting my marriage proposal.

Dan Zevin

When we hosted Thanksgiving at our house in Brooklyn last year, my wife and I toiled to follow in the footsteps of her parents. Much like the Puritans, we applied our work ethic to acquiring, preparing, and presenting the Bird the hard way. The New England way. Which probably explains why we'll be introducing our kids to a new Thanksgiving tradition this year. Here in New Amsterdam, it's known as the Caterer.

The Day I Turned into My Father

"A man should never stop learning, even on his last day," my father tells me. "Maimonides." We're at the entrance to Costco in Union, New Jersey. He's about to demonstrate how to maximize the cargo space of the wide-load shopping carts he has hand-selected for us. "Observe," he says. And with a flick of the wrist, he expands the folding baby seat.

"But why?" I ask. "Why must we expand these baby seats when the kids are at your house watching Animal Planet with our wives?"

"All in good time my boy, all in good time. Cervantes."

When the glass doors slide open, I experience a pre-vomit, fight-or-flight sensation. My vision is blurred by an onslaught of flashing, flat-panel screens. A man tries to make me eat free samples of crabmeat salad on a cracker. A guard chases me down, demanding to see my membership card. She notices my father, sorting through his circular.

"Dr. Zevin! I was wondering when you were coming!"

My father knows the bouncer. I can relax.

"I tied her tubes three weeks ago," he tells me, striding by with a smile. As we make our way in, he smiles and waves to several other personnel he seems to know intimately, and most likely does, since he is their gynecologist.

"Follow me," my father says. "Wait'll you see the bananas they got back there. My treat."

Lately all my friends are worried that they're turning into their fathers. I'm worried that I'm not. My father is calm, cool, and collected. I am tense, clammy, and confused. My father has interests and hobbies, including numismatics, philosophy, karaoke, and planning his high school reunion. I no longer give a shit about any activity that's not preceded by the phrase *after-school*. My father wants nothing more than to be needed. He spends eight hours a day providing sliding-scale services to underprivileged patients in Newark, New Jersey. I want nothing more than to be less needed. I spend eight minutes a day providing nauseatingly upbeat content to OldMan.com (latest blog: "Your Babysitter Has a Crush on You. Really!"). Above all, my dad is Dr. Generosity. With each passing year, he's become more of a giver. And I . . . well, I've become more of a taker. A taker of the toilet paper twelve-packs he gives me, the casks of Cascade he gives me, the tallboys of Pledge he gives me. I used to think of myself as a self-sufficient guy, believe it or not. But these days, I think of myself as . . .

Sorry, it appears I've lost track of how I think of myself these days. These days, I think of my family. And my dog, and my town house, and my minivan, which got sideswiped by a street-sweeping truck in the middle of the night last week, and also I think we're out of frozen shrimp, and I think Megan said she has to work late tonight, so I have to cook dinner for the kids, and by "cook dinner," I mean "defrost a fistful of frozen shrimp."

These days, I think of myself as a guy who will take whatever the hell he can get. Including another plastic duffel bag of frozen shrimp that I need to remind my father to give me.

I never used to dwell upon where my father got all the stuff he gave me. As far as I was concerned, it came from his basement, the onetime site of my childhood playroom before he re-envisioned it as a way station stacked from linoleum floor to stucco ceiling with his provisions. I mean, I was aware, obviously, that he acquired it all from his number one travel destination—quite a distinction, considering numbers two and three (seriously) are the Metropolitan Museum of Art and the American Museum of Natural History. He called it the "club." For years I'd rebuffed invitations to be a guest at his club. But I'd been fielding the phone calls about twice a week.

"Danny, I'm at the club. Whaddaya need?"

"Let me call you back, Dad. Josie's got my stapler in her mouth."

"Perfect. I'll get you a shipping crate of Band-Aids. And it sounds like she's gonna need a Waterpik."

"Dad, she still has her baby teeth."

"It's not for her teeth. It's for her gums."

This year, I finally decided to show my dad how grateful I was to have a give-and-take relationship in which he gives and I take. So I joined him on a bonding expedition neither one of us will soon forget. It was not a father-son fishing trip (though I did come home with a dozen tins of boneless sockeye salmon with 410 milligrams of omega-3s per serving). We did not spend the afternoon out on the court (though I now possess a six-pack of cushioned tennis socks). Ours was an epic adventure, a classic rite of passage in which an uninitiated acolyte is summoned into the unknown to learn at the feet of the elder.

Little did I know it then, but I was about to embark on a journey that would bring me one step closer to my goal of being Ronald Zevin, provider. Instead of Dan Zevin, providee.

I was spellbound by a tank of orange Utz cheese balls when my father tapped me on the shoulder. "Monosodium glutamate," he solemnly said, leading me away from the cheese balls and over to a vessel of All-Natural Veggie Crunchers. We'd been in Costco for fifteen minutes, and already his cart contained the U.S. recommended daily, and yearly, allowance of bananas. "Have you ever seen bananas like these, Danny?" he inquired, holding his harvest high in the air. It was a rhetorical question. He grabbed a bunch—eighty or so—and carefully placed them into my cart, along with a mile-long vine of red seedless grapes and the gross national product of Nova Scotia in blueberries.

"To lengthen thy life, lessen thy meals," my father declared. "Benjamin Franklin."

This is how my father talks. In sayings. Walking around Costco with him was like walking around Costco with the author of *Bartlett's Familiar Quotations* (who would be Bartlett, I'm guessing). But Ronald's familiar quotations are way more familiar, at least to his offspring. Over the course of the next few miles, he quoted Gandhi, Einstein, da Vinci, DiMaggio, Jung, and Allen (Woody). Quote-wise, Allen has always been his go-to source. Growing up, my shy sister, Ally, was told over and over, "You have to have a little faith in people," which she knew at age nine was the last line of *Manhattan*. When my older brother, Barry (aka the one who got the brains), announced he was switching his major at Columbia from pre-med to World Religions, my father reacted as follows: "Not only is there no God, but try getting a plumber on weekends. Chapter four, *Getting Even*." As for me, 100 percent of my quotes were of the "Don't worry, be happy" / "Don't sweat the small stuff" / "Keep calm, carry on" variety, so it's not surprising that I never got

Allen. The most memorable saying he gave me came on my Bar Mitzvah, when he was called to the pulpit to provide fatherly advice. It was from a Rudyard Kipling poem called "If." "If you can keep your head when all about you are losing theirs . . . you'll be a Man, my son."

Based on that benchmark, I never became a man. But it wasn't until answering my father's clarion call to Costco that I suddenly identified the real roadblock. He was standing in aisle 4,000-B with an ear-to-ear grin and a shrink-wrapped 60-pack of paper towels. Tactfully, he removed himself from the embrace of a supervisor whose name tag read Esther, and upon whom he had recently performed a pap smear. The time had come for him to reveal the secrets of the expandable child seat.

As he instructed, I flipped down the plastic red covering, thus blocking the leg holes. Words were not necessary as he presented me with paper towels. He merely motioned with his chin to put them where the child goes. It was uncanny; a precise fit.

"A new type of thinking is essential if mankind is to survive," my father remarked. "Albert Einstein."

I appreciate my father's generosity, I really do. And I really do wish to emulate his confidence, his level-headedness, his ability to "keep calm and carry on" without the use of anti-anxiety medication. But something about the paper towel situation made me see what I had to do to *be* the kind of man my father is. Like Odysseus, son of Laertes, I had to break away. Just like Homer will tell you, it's hard to feel like a man when you're in your forties and your dad is still buying you paper towels.

Adrenaline coursed through my veins, though I knew not what lay ahead. "Excuse me, Dad, I have to go find some things for the kids," I said. And with that, I boldly set forth on my solo sojourn toward a barrel of ChapStick. But first, I agreed to follow him to aisle 9,999, where we were treated to unlimited French toast sticks by the lovely Rosaria ("fibroids," whispered my father).

How I wound up getting my eyes examined remains a mystery. One minute I was inspecting a steamer tank of T-shirts, the next I was weighing the pros and cons of stackable washer-dryers, then there I was, reading an eye chart in the Costco optometrist's office. I still don't know what happened. I think I just got swept up in the thrill of discovering that Costco even *has* an optometrist, much less one who's rocking the long white lab coat and all.

To be honest, this kind of attention-deficit shopping is par for my course. To give you an idea of me in the open market, imagine a kid in a candy store. Now imagine that kid has juvenile diabetes. Unlike my father, who can zero in on a carton of nine-volt batteries the way a skilled hunter can sense his prey, I can barely walk into a supermarket without being paralyzed by all the peanut butter. Until I figured out how to do online grocery shopping, I'd stand in the store for ten minutes trying to choose between Jif or Skippy, smooth or crunchy, normal or nasty (that kind with the peanut juice floating around on top). Finally, I'd come to a firm decision. "Today I'll just get jelly," I'd firmly decide. "Tomorrow, I'll come back for the peanut butter." And if I chickened out, so what? It was only a matter of time until a shipment of peanut butter would be provided by the patriarch, care of his club.

I never considered it a shortcoming, actually. Prior to my Costco-induced identity crisis, I thought of consumer culture as shallow and wasteful. Wasn't I the guy who spent his adult life distancing himself from Exit 7C (the Short Hills

Mall)? Wasn't I the guy who married a girl from New Hampshire instead of New Jersey, a girl for whom outdoor recreation was not synonymous with sidewalk sales? Together, we chose to raise our kids among the reducers, reusers, and recyclers of Brooklyn, where big-box stores are dismissed not only as category killers, but something worse: community-killers. In Brooklyn, we have one mom-and-pop store for cheese, another for chocolate, and another for bread. When we first moved here, it felt like shopping in Europe. Now it feels like shopping in Europe when the international exchange rate is at an all-time low. But that's the price you pay for living in a place with character. Instead of a place with Costco.

I spotted the Guinness World Records holder for biggest piece of seasoned, breaded tilapia in aisle 43,000. It was the same price as a single popcorn shrimp at our neighborhood fishmonger in Brooklyn. Foraging on, I found a Flintstones-size sirloin for $1.99 a pound. If my math was correct, this meant I could get the whole cow for the cost of some meatballs at my butcher in Cobble Hill. But where would I put these supersized foodstuffs even if I *was* kind of, sort of coming around to the economics involved? I'd need a second fridge (aisle 938) like the one my father keeps in his basement, along with boxes of Brillo fit for a Warhol installation, toothpaste in tubes meant for contractor's caulk, and Janitor in a Drum jugs large enough to be taken literally.

Seriously, where would I put all this stuff even if I *was* kind of, sort of coming around to the convenience of purchasing all of one's products under one roof, instead of schlepping around Brooklyn to the Brillo store, the toothpaste monger, and that funky Janitor in a Drum boutique in Williamsburg? Unlike the spacious suburban home where my old air hockey table is now being used to display the world's foremost collection of Kirkland-brand merchandise, our twenty-foot-wide town house—the Taj Mahal by Brooklyn standards—is at overflow capacity. Under Josie's bed is where we keep all the Kleenex (that my father gave me). Behind the pedestal of the pedestal sink is where we stack up the vitamins (that my father gave me). I can't even recline anymore in my reclining, swiveling chair. The last time I tried, I smashed into a tower of diet dog food cans (that my father gave me). (And my mother returned to Costco after visiting us last Tuesday. She tossed ten dented cans in her purse—trust me, they fit—convinced they were tainted with botulism.)

As for all other inventory, it travels as cargo in my minivan. My father didn't give me the minivan. He did, however, urge me to buy it myself via the vehicle purchasing program available exclusively to members of his club. I got out of that one with a quote of my own. "I refuse to join any club that would have me as a member," I said to my dad with a wink. "Woody Allen."

"Woody Allen didn't say that," my father replied. "Groucho Marx said that."

But none of that mattered on my vision quest through Costco. Suddenly, I was overcome by a powerful, nearly primal pull toward a double-wide flat of Poland Spring mini bottles. It seemed to me we were running low the last time I looked in the fireplace. Yes. I distinctly remembered writing this verbatim reminder on the dry erase board (that my father gave me): *More Poland Spring mini bottles (tell Dad)*. But where was Dad now? Probably in the pharmacy department, chatting up some well-wishers he was treating for chlamydia. If I wished to replenish my family's water supply, it was up to me now. Seizing my conquest from the shelf, the wisdom of the elder echoed in my mind: "Use the rack *underneath* your shopping cart for oversized flats, Danny. Most people don't even know that's what it's there for."

With the water beneath my cart, I had completed a critical step in my initiation. I was on my way to becoming a provider.

Of course there were life-changing discoveries along the way. There was the discovery of the "Zibra Open It!" pruning shears I'd later use to pry out the Fusion ProGlide Power and MicroComb razor blades that were packed in bulletproof plastic. There was the discovery of expandable colanders—*expandable*—which expand over a man's sink to wash the fruits, vegetables, and grains he provides for his family. (Except the single-ton serving size of cherry tomatoes, because, if you believe the label, they were already triple washed.) And finally, there was the discovery of Craisins. Did you know there exists in nature a food that is a combination of cranberries and raisins? Me neither. But at Costco, I gathered enough of the succulent berries to last my family through the brutal Brooklyn winter that lay ahead.

By the time my cart was three-quarters full—which I know sounds impressive, but the assortment of Kirkland handcrafted Hefferveisen, amber ale, German lager, and pale ale took up nearly half of it—a sense of inner peace had replaced my Shopper's ADD. This is how my father feels all the time, I reflected. Because of his relationship with Costco, he is not preoccupied with the threat of carbon monoxide in his home, since he knows exactly where to get a Nighthawk two-pack carbon monoxide detector (from aisle 60½). Blackouts don't bother him because he has access to candles with on-off switches instead of just wicks. Safety pins, rubber bands, twisty-ties, hangers—all of those things a person never buys, but somehow still has—they all can be traced back to Costco.

Thanks to my father, I now understood: A man can't attain the enlightened state of Provider until he knows all that is possible to provide.

Armed with insight, I felt increasingly focused. Instead of bouncing around like a pinball from floor coverings to Q-Tips, I learned that each purchase should lead logically to the next. I'd have to say I hit my stride with the Little Giant M17 MegaLite Ladder. Not to brag, but my thought process was perfectly linear:

a. Oh look, there is a case of lightbulbs like the one that's burned out in the living room ceiling.

b. The reason I left it burned out is because it's a hassle to reach it on our shitty little stepladder.

c. In order to reach it, I must obtain that MegaLite Ladder over there by the fire extinguishers.

d. Speaking of fire extinguishers, we should have some of those.

e. The answer is yes, we do need battery-operated smoke alarms. Our hardwired ones go off the second you light a candle.

f. Which is why I am getting these candles with the on-off switch.

g. Huh. Why would they stock fifteen-pound buckets of cake icing right next to the radon detectors?

I drew the line at the cake icing. Even as a provider, I could see that a fifteen-pound bucket of cake icing was one thing I didn't need to provide.

h. Maybe next spring, when the kids have their birthdays.

When I returned to my father, he was inspecting a karaoke machine with an employee (C-section) who looked like Queen Latifah. As he surveyed the spoils of my well-stocked cart, his face beamed with pride. It was an expression I have rarely seen. I know you are shocked. But when your father's a lifelong provider, you get precious few chances to make him feel proud. You might even suspect that the real reason he's providing is that he thinks you can't do it yourself. Deep down, there's not a doubt in my mind that my father is proud of me. But sometimes I wonder if it's not only pride that he's feeling, but pride laced with pity.

My mind drifted back to a time long ago. My second book had just been published. It was a satirical guide for couples about to be wed, subtitled "How to Survive the Happiest Day of Your Life." The happiest day of my father's life was the day he saw my book displayed at Papyrus, the fancy stationery store ranking right up there with his club and his museums on his list of best-loved travel destinations. Why Papyrus is hard to say. I imagine the greeting cards there give him a lot of material for his proverbs. In any case, he called me the second he got home from the mall.

"Danny, they had your book in Papyrus! A whole stack. I bought every one."

"Wow, thanks, Dad."

"I told the lady you wrote it. She was very impressed."

"Thanks."

"Nice lady. She said she'd be willing to take a meeting with us."

I could see where this was going. My father wanted me to do a book signing at his beloved Papyrus.

"As it happens, Papyrus is a franchise. Do you know what I mean by a franchise, Danny?"

The pride part was ending.

"A franchise means the lady *owns* the Papyrus. And let me tell you something, she does very well for herself."

The pity had begun.

"So now that you and Megan will be settling down and starting a family, maybe it's time that you'd like to—"

"Do a book signing at Papyrus?"

"Oh. Sure. Wonderful idea. But also, *open* a Papyrus."

Gazing upon my cart at Costco all these years later, my father was all pride, no pity. But I had a bad feeling he was about to ask me to try the karaoke machine with him. Asking me to sing karaoke with him was something he'd been doing ever since my siblings and I gave a command performance of "Papa Was a Rolling Stone" at the seventieth birthday throwdown we had for him. And, frankly, singing karaoke once every seventy years seemed like an ideal schedule to me. Or to the old me, I should say—the inhibited, uptight one who had not yet conquered Costco with his father. But now, here, today, everything was different. My father and I had become equals; not a father and a son, but two fathers together—he with his cart of bananas, me with my MegaLite Ladder. The result was an electrifying, father-son duet of "Bye-Bye Miss American Pie."

When a man is a provider, you must understand, he wants to break out in song.

Outside, the sun was setting, and the time had finally come to face my final challenge before checking out: the membership desk. It was there that my father introduced me to Lucille (yeast infection), who used her employee privileges to upgrade me to an Executive Membership. My father took out his wallet.

"No, Dad," I insisted. "Allow me."

Not long from now, our roles will reverse and I'll be the one providing for him. I'll provide a 76-count case of Depends, a Medline deluxe rolling walker with built-in cup holder, a 30-pack of hearing aid batteries in a choice of orange, brown, or yellow. And, when his time comes, I'll provide him with the one final item we found by the exit doors. It was the Costco coffin. My father quoted Woody Allen as soon as he saw it. "I'm not afraid of death," he said. " I just don't want to be there when it happens." When it does, though, I'm pretty sure I know where he'd like to be buried.

I shall bring my son, Leo, to Costco one day, and Leo shall bring his son, and the patriarchal cycle of Zevin providers shall forever continue. In the meantime, I decided to spring for the bananas. Handing my Executive Membership ID to the cashier (vaginitis), it struck me that you don't really know what you look like until you've seen your digitized face on the back of a Costco card. On mine, I'm the spitting image of my dad.

Suburbed:
Scenes from a Summer Vacation

I'm locked out of my locker at the town pool

I'm wearing a wet bathing suit, goggles, and SpongeBob flip-flops I stole from the Lost and Found. I've just finished swimming laps. Correction: swimming lap. Don't overdo the physical therapy, my knee surgeon warned. So I'm not over-doing it. I'm just standing outside my locker, thinking about everything locked up inside. My clothes. My wallet. The key to my minivan. The key to my locker. A clock near the snack bar says it's 2:45. I have fifteen minutes to pick up my kids. They're at day camp. It's their first day.

"This is embarrassing, but I locked my key inside my locker," I tell the girl at the desk. She looks eighteen. But I'm sure she has a lock-cutting apparatus, one of those giant hedge clippers the lifeguards always used back in Brooklyn when some-one got locked out at the Red Hook Pool. This was before they found out about the guys pretending to be locked out so they could steal all the stuff in someone else's locker.

"Apparatus?" the girl says to me. "What do you mean? What kind of apparatus?"

When the fire engine pulls up, all the kids at the town pool rush over to the fence. They think there's a fire. But the fireman doesn't have a hose. He has an apparatus. A lock-cutting apparatus that looks like giant hedge clippers.

He's a nice fireman. He doesn't look at me funny because he is wearing a firefighting uniform and I am wearing Lost and Found flip-flops. He is a fireman of few words.

"You're from the city," he says. It's not a question. He just knows.

And then:

"You don't have to lock here."

We are living in another family's house

Which comes with their driveway, their yard, their furniture, their DVDs, their Wii, and their town pool. We're here courtesy of craigslist, summer rentals, keyword: central air-conditioning.

One summer earlier. Brooklyn. Megan and I take a vow. We vow to get central air-conditioning. Megan does a cost analysis. It'll be cheaper to rent a summer house every summer for the next ten summers than it will be to get central air-conditioning. We're not enjoying ourselves. We're not having the Summer of Love. We're having the Summer of Sam, named in honor of our latest neighbor, Sam, who's renting a room in the town house attached to ours. It seems that Sam's caseworkers have concluded—incorrectly—that he no longer requires twenty-four-hour observation by licensed professionals. Sam takes his crazy pill every night at 2 a.m. He spends the subsequent hours screaming very bad words at his girlfriend. One night, the domestic violence unit shows up. They tell us don't worry. It turns out his "girlfriend" is actually a computer monitor. Until he can be evicted, they have a solution. We should close our windows.

So we revise our vow. We vow to rent a summer house. A *real* house. A house that isn't preceded by the word "town" or "row," and isn't "attached" or "semidetached" to any neighboring town houses or row houses, and isn't next door to any neighboring neighbors who are *completely* detached (from reality). Our children will fall asleep to the sound of crickets instead of the sound of Tourette's. They'll attend a day camp conducted in the out-of-doors, where they won't sit in a classroom watching *Pocahontas II* on the nicest day of August "because the air quality advisory prevented our playground work today," according to the Montessori-certified counselor where they went the summer before. And they'll play freeze tag somewhere more scenic than the Astroturf schoolyard at PS 38, landscaped with broken glass and family planning products.

We have a plan. We are ecstatic. Every conflicted feeling we've ever had about raising kids in the city will be resolved by our summer rental house. All we have to do now is find one.

What my mother says

The condo next door to mine in Bradley Beach! Lenore's gonna rent it out this year to pay for her lips. You'll all spend the summer with me and Bob in New Jersey!

What my father says

A penny saved is a penny earned. Why don't you stay here, for free, with me and Bebe? A deal like this doesn't come along every day in Short Hills, New Jersey!

Dan Zevin

So here we are in Westchester, New York

The Hamptons have the beaches. The Berkshires have the mountains. But Katonah has the commute: fifty-eight climate-controlled minutes on the Metro-North Railroad to Megan's job in the city. So I get back on craigslist. I find a family to move into our town house in Brooklyn, and I find a family to rent us their suburban house in Westchester. All I bring for myself are some clothes and my laptop. What else do I need? I'm a writer. The way I see it, there are just as many ways to avoid writing in the suburbs as there are in the city. Maybe more.

Take swimming, for example

After a few weeks, I develop a routine. Each morning, I take the kids to camp, then drive to the town pool. But something surprising happens. I like it. The quiet, I mean. Underwater, I am reminded, there is no sound. Nothing has been this quiet for years. For six and three-quarters years, to be exact. *Why, isn't that a peculiar coincidence?* I think to myself one morning while doing the crawl. *That is exactly the same number of years it has been since I became a parent.*

Anyway, I get sort of hooked on the quiet. I start needing it. For me, quiet is the new loud. And maybe it's because of the quiet, or maybe it's because of the lack of oxygen uptake to my cerebral cortex, but one morning while I'm quietly crawling, I start thinking something crazy. I start thinking maybe this is the summer I'll be capable of giving a shit again. About writing, I mean. Enough already with this nauseatingly upbeat blog, I'm thinking while I'm quietly crawling. Why not spend the summer writing something new, something challenging, something I've always wanted to write but never knew how?

A movie. Yes, that is it. This summer, I will both do laps and complete a major motion picture. I've got it all figured out by my fifth (i.e., final) lap. It's about a guy who gets a minivan because he thinks he's outgrown his car. But by the end of the movie, he realizes he's outgrown his life. And any resemblance to real persons living or dead will be purely coincidental.

Whatever I do, I won't go to Starbucks

The article in the local giveaway paper is called "The 10 Top-Notchiest, Totally Awesomest, Family-Friendliest Towns Around." I find it in a stack at Petite Patisserie, where I should really be reading the copy of *Screenwriting for Dummies* I've checked out of the library. Let me say something about this library. My kids can't get over it. The chairs aren't sticky. The fish aren't floating at the top of the tank. The librarian doesn't say all the books they want are out on "perma-loan," as they like to put it at the Pacific Street branch back in Brooklyn. Later today, I'll bring my kids to "storytime before suppertime," where I will be the token dad. But now they're at camp. And Megan is at work. And I'm in Petite Patisserie, where I really should be reading *Screenwriting for Dummies*.

"Are you an artsy-craftsy urban expat craving a heaping mug of creative stimulation?" the giveaway paper is asking me. "Then you'll love the '*buzz*' at Dragonfly Coffeehouse in Pleasantville." I look around at the Polo-clad clientele in Petite Patisserie. They don't strike me as particularly artsy, though I guess the majority of them could be considered craftsy since they're constructing Popsicle stick jewelry boxes with the art teacher from Little Picassos. But at least it's not Starbucks, I tell myself. Starbucks is a little *too* suburban-sterile for an emerging movie writer and lap swimmer such as myself. For the rest of the summer, my position on Starbucks will remain firm: takeout, not hangout.

The lady in the tight tennis dress

So off I go. Day after day, I drive around suburban Westchester with *Screenwriting for Dummies* and my laptop, searching for some funky, indie coffeehouse like the Flying Saucer back in Brooklyn. The Flying Saucer is a beat-up couch, Belle & Sebastian situation providing free office space for freelancers half my age and a hundred times more ambitious. *If only I can find Westchester's version of the Flying Saucer,* I convince myself, *I will get those creative juices flowing once more. Perhaps it is a franchise, like Papyrus.*

The Dragonfly place in Pleasantville comes close, as promised by the free local paper I am still carting around. It has rice paper lanterns instead of regular lights. But it's empty. Worse, the radio is on, and it's playing "That's Just the Way It Is" by Bruce Hornsby and the Range.

Days go by. My search for a heaping mug of creative stimulation continues. An empty café in Bedford that is housed in a Kundalini yoga studio: I read *Screenwriting for Dummies* surrounded by shelves stocked with hemp eye pillows. An empty café in Tarrytown that is next to a concert hall where Bruce Hornsby and the Range are probably playing tonight: I read *Screenwriting for Dummies* while the floor is mopped with Pine-Sol. A semi-empty café in a strip mall in Croton: I read

Screenwriting for Dummies while being stared down by my fellow customer. She's a middle-aged woman wearing a cleavagey white tennis dress. Her cup has lipstick on it. I know this because she puts it on my table.

"Are you a screenwriter?" she says.

"Sort of," I say.

"Sort of?" she says. "That's like saying you're sort of married."

It is?, I think. But I don't say anything. I'm a little scared of her.

"Well, are you?" she asks.

"Yeah, I am," I answer.

"Good," she says, "'cuz I am, too. Sort of married."

Starbucks: could be worse

The one in Mt. Kisco has these special iTunes cards they give out every Tuesday. You just type in the special code on your card, and you get a free download. A dark curtain has lifted. All those years I spent wondering how anyone of my advanced age keeps up with what the kids are listening to these days. I'm finally in on their little secret.

So here's what happens. I become a regular. Every Tuesday, I sit in my lucky armchair, listen to my Starbucks Pick of the Week, and work on my movie about the fictional guy who gets the minivan. And every Tuesday, I notice another regular with whom I have something in common. We're the only members of our gender who don't come here with our mommies. Though the only reason mine isn't here is because she's picking up the kids from camp and taking them to be screened for Lyme disease.

There's something else this guy and I have in common. We're both wearing high-tops instead of wingtips. And his Elvis Costello glasses pretty much confirm what I've suspected since he became my imaginary best friend a few weeks ago: He, too, is an artsy-craftsy urban expat craving a heaping mug of creative stimulation. I wind up standing in line behind him one morning. He, too, cringes when he has to say "venti." I recognize myself in him.

Lo and behold. He recognizes me, too.

"You look familiar," he says. "Oh yeah, aren't you that guy who got locked out at the pool?"

He is Pete. He moved here from the city. He is having a fortieth birthday barbecue. I should bring the family.

I've made my first suburban friend.

My son is up a tree

Megan and I are watching him from the family room window, transfixed. We can't believe it. He's been in the tree for like twelve straight minutes. He climbed it yesterday, too, and the day before that. Sometimes the kid across the street comes over, and they climb it together. Then they just sit in it. They just sit in the tree. They don't even try to push each other off.

This is not how outdoor recreation is conducted back in Brooklyn. In Brooklyn, there is a compelling argument for population control known as Carroll Park. Carroll Park is the kind of full-occupancy destination that's all fun and games until your children are trampled to death. One day, I remember telling my kids, that's it—no more playing in the playground part of Carroll Park. So we check out the rest of the park. We find a quiet garden. It has some trees and a big rock.

Leo climbs one of the trees. He's happy up there. He's content. Next thing I know, he's in tears. An old lady with a mustache and an apron that says "Carroll Park Greening Committee" is yelling at him to get down. I tell her to relax, and she starts yelling at me.

"Your children are not supposed to be climbing trees!" she says.

Sometimes when Megan and I are watching Leo from our family room window, I think about that old hag.

Your children are not supposed to be climbing trees.

If I knew then what I know now, this is what I would have said:

Yes they are.

My wife is on a train

She's coming home from work. She is seated. She is serene. She is traveling at sea level. It's early August now, and Megan exudes good commuter karma. A month has passed since she was emancipated from the New York City subway system. This evening, like every evening, she will pull into the train station at 6:18, where she'll be greeted on the platform by her loving husband and devoted children. When I ask how her day was, she will not say: "The guy standing next to me on the subway picked his nose and wiped the boogie on the pole I was holding." Instead, she will utter one single word, and that word will be: *wonderful.*

So the four of us will walk home together, to another family's house. We'll play freeze tag together, in another family's yard. We'll eat dinner together, on another family's deck. And then, once the kids are asleep, there is a strong likelihood that Megan and I will engage in marital relations together, in another family's bed. Which will be located in another family's master bedroom—the spacious, suburban kind with wall-to-wall carpeting instead of wall-to-wall bed—and this master bedroom will be a huge turn-on for us, and the earth will move.

My daughter is in a show

There's an old song from Carole King's *Really Rosie* album that becomes the soundtrack to our summer. It's called "My Simple Humble Neighborhood." Josie's group has to perform it at the big end-of-camp show. When the day finally comes, Megan and I get to the barn early to score front-row seats. The song has become background music after six weeks in heavy rotation. But witnessing the Mini-Midgets' live version is unforgettable.

> *In my simple humble neighborhood,*
> *On my simple humble street . . .*

Josie looks insanely cute through the lens of my minicam. Inside, though, here's what I'm thinking: Wow, she is really full of shit.

What I mean is, Josie is the only mini-midget who's faking it up there. *She* doesn't live in a simple, humble neighborhood on a simple humble street. She lives in a crowded, gentrifying neighborhood in the most densely populated borough of New York. Gentrify-*ING*, meaning the ratio of bail bond offices to organic, free-range ice cream shops in her humble little neighborhood is now about 1:3.

Seemed like a good idea at the time

It's the summer of 2002. Megan and I have just moved to Brooklyn. We find our dream home: a cozy, brick town house in a gentrifying neighborhood of Brooklyn. Gentrify-*ING*, meaning the ratio of bail bond offices to organic, free-range ice cream shops is still about 3:1. But the important thing is, the ice cream is to die for. Our only dependent is a dog, and Chloe couldn't be happier with all the new sights to see, people to meet, places to pee. We couldn't agree with her more. We're Yuppies in love, and we live in the coolest city on earth. There's a bistro a few blocks away called Robin des Bois. They have a taxidermy crocodile and a pinball machine, and a funky backyard where we drink pitchers of Brooklyn Lager. Everyone we meet is incredibly friendly and interesting and a freelance graphic designer. That December, we buy all our holiday gifts at Brooklyn Industries. It's like The Gap, but hipper. Their motto is "Live, Work, Create." We're going to live here forever.

A few years pass. We're not Yuppies anymore. We're just Uppies. We're still in love, we've just begun expressing it in a more . . . irritable fashion since the two of us turned into the four of us. People start asking if we're going to stay in Brooklyn. We're puzzled by this question. We're city people, we tell them, and Brooklyn has everything a family could want. Where else can you walk out your front door and find a five-piece Mariachi band playing outside some new empanada place? A street fair celebrating not just Memorial Day but *Bastille* Day? A real-life Sesame Street where kids grow up in stimulating, diverse communities instead of sheltered, vanilla suburbs?

The *SUB*urbs. After a few years in Brooklyn, we learn to

stress the first syllable. All the dads are absentee fathers. All the moms are desperate housewives. You have to drive everywhere. The taxes will kill you, and if they don't, a vicious deer in your backyard will. The toddlers are addicted to Halo; the teenagers are drunk drivers; the neighbors are known sex offenders. There's nothing to do and nowhere to go. And don't get me started on the bagels.

The last thing left to gentrify

One day while glancing at a calendar, I discover that five or six years seem to have transpired. A few blocks from our town house, a trendy hotel has opened directly across the street from the Brooklyn House of Detention. We joke that this is excellent news for the prisoners. Now if they make bail, they can celebrate by going out for an organic, free-range, reclaimed, locally sourced, shade-grown sundae and spending the night in a $300 hotel room the same size as their cell.

The one thing left to gentrify in our neighborhood is our neighborhood school. The Department of Education has released something called School Report Cards. Our neighborhood school does not exactly pass with flying colors. Leo's supposed to start kindergarten there in the fall. So we begin exploring schools in other neighborhoods. Exploring schools in other neighborhoods becomes our full-time job. We explore charter schools, magnet schools, Waldorf schools, bridge schools, inclusion schools, and private—sorry, *independent*—schools. We sign waiting lists, apply for variances, enter lotteries, request exemptions, go on tours. We visit schools with "gifted and talented" programs and schools with "special needs" programs.

"Everyone applies as special needs," whispers a parent I run into at a public school called The Children's School, which supposedly does admissions by lottery. "That way, you get three teachers in one room. Just say your kid needs speech therapy. That qualifies."

Leo eventually gets into one (1) school. And not because I pretend he needs speech therapy. He doesn't get into *any* of the schools where I pretend he needs speech therapy. He gets in off the waiting list. He lucks out. And so do we. With our son in a good public school, we can relax. We can relax for exactly two years, because that's when our daughter starts school. The "sibling policy," we learn, does not automatically cover families who live outside the zone. The irony doesn't escape us. After months spent navigating the city's byzantine admissions process, we already feel zoned out. In two more years, we might be able to make it official.

This is what we tell ourselves. We'll cross that bridge when we come to it. After all, this is The City, and we are part of something *special*. Here, our kids can get a *real* education, not just a classroom education like they'd get in the *SUB*urbs. Here, there are museums, and theater, and, hmmm . . . let's see . . . organic, free-range ice cream! And artisanal, Rainforest Alliance–certified, cruelty-free pizza, and single-press, vacuum-brewed, multiracial espresso, and . . . what else? Robin des Bois! Yes, Brooklyn is *full* of cool bars like Robin des Bois, and that's actually very important for children when you think about it, because all the interesting, creative people hang out in cool bars, and it can only be good for kids to absorb all that creativity, right? And it's good for them to be able to walk everywhere, too. Because walking builds up their leg muscles, especially when they break into a wild sprint down Atlantic Avenue like ours do, narrowly averting their daily hit-and-run by the kamikaze driver of bus 63 to Park Slope. Which probably wouldn't be such a bad thing anyway, because the only way children learn is from firsthand experience, so getting hit by a bus will be an important part of their education—a *teaching moment*. Little kids aren't even *exposed* to public transportation in the *SUB*urbs, we tell ourselves. But ours will ride the subway to school every day, and this will give them extra reading practice, because they'll be given the opportunity to sound out public service posters like the one on the F train that reads, "A Crowded Subway Train Is No Excuse for Unlawful Sexual Conduct." And once they learn to read it, we can explain what it means, so, boom, that's another teaching moment right there. Spending their childhoods in Brooklyn will make our kids street-smart, not just book-smart, we tell ourselves. And that, we tell ourselves, is going to give them a huge advantage over all those sheltered, shallow children from . . .

The suburbs: could be worse

My new suburban friend Pete has the most magnificent Weber gas barbecue grill I have ever laid eyes on. It has four stainless steel burners *plus* a flush-mounted side burner, and when you lift the lid, the whole thing lights up the way a refrigerator does when you open the door. As a matter of fact, this grill is the size of a refrigerator. And the kabobs emerging from it are truly kabobs from another world. Everyone at Pete's fortieth-birthday barbecue is having fun. The kids are jumping on the trampoline and running around the backyard. His wife is walking Megan around the patio to meet the neighbors. It's not a huge house by suburban standards, but there've got to be at least seventy-five people here. And here's the thing. They all fit.

As the evening winds down, Megan and I find ourselves in a group of couples who all moved here from Manhattan or Brooklyn. Each seems to have some melodramatic moment that led them to flee the city. A mugging; a slumlord; a fight for a cab leading a professional woman in pearls to shout, "I was here first, you bitch!" The woman telling us the story confesses that she was the one in the pearls. She tells us that's when she knew it was time for a lifestyle change.

When it's Pete's turn to share, here's all he says: "We spent the first few years trying to fit the kids into our lives, so now it's our turn to fit into theirs."

I find this sentence profound.

Then Max comes to town

Actually, he does more than come to town. He comes to the town pool. He comes with his wife, Kim, and their six-year-old, Shane. We've been next-door neighbors for years now, ever since our boys were babies vying for the attention of the original hipster nanny, Stephanie. Max and I have managed to stay friends through playdates and double dates, but it's taken six weeks to convince him to drive out from Brooklyn before the pool closes for the season. Max is a born-and-bred New Yorker. He doesn't really like getting wet.

By now, the pool has become my second summer home. I'm up to twenty laps. I don't lock. Sometimes, the girl at the front desk doesn't make me show my nonresident summer tenant pass. We're that close.

Max is wearing black cut-offs, a black T-shirt, and a snug black ski cap. It's 80 degrees. Kim works in fashion. She's wearing a form-fitting bikini that looks like it's made out of balloon rubber. Shane only stands out for what he's *not* wearing: a special, quick-drying swimming shirt from the Land's End catalog. He has a tank top from Brooklyn Industries. It says "Live, Work, Create."

The townspeople are staring. Really, they are. I'm trying to ignore it as I lead them to our usual spot by the tennis courts. But, inside, I'm imagining the scene through their sheltered suburban eyes. We're surrounded by a fog of hashish smoke, accompanied by the blaring beat of "Fuck tha Police" by N.W.A. Kim is balancing the boom box on her shoulder. Max is packing spray paint instead of sunscreen. Shane is hell-bent on defacing some municipal property. "Suburbia Sucks," he's going to scrawl over the "Rules For Proper Conduct" sign posted by the snack bar.

When we finally spread our picnic blanket out, part of me is still feeling self-conscious. On the bright side, I'm thinking this will make a funny scene in my major motion picture one day.

Or a really depressing one, depending on your point of view

By which I mean: Max's point of view. From Max's point of view, the town pool is not a fun place to spend the afternoon. I'm pretty sure this is what he means when he says, "It's not even a pool, it's a cesspool. A cesspool of suburban lethargy."

Max shares his opinion at exactly four o'clock. I know this for a fact because four o'clock is when Adult Swim occurs. All six lifeguards blow their whistles at the same time, and the kids obediently dog-paddle to the sides and climb out. But the weird thing is this. The adults don't swim. They float. The same dozen or so adults every time. The girl at the front desk hands them these fancy white rafts that look like yoga mats, and they spend the next fifteen minutes luxuriating in the deep end while all the kids wait anxiously to get back in. Megan and I have never participated in Adult Swim. We're usually too busy trying to get Leo and Josie to stop crying because they had to get out of the pool.

"You've got to be fucking kidding me," Max says.

"I know, it's a little weird," I say.

"No, it's more than a little weird," Max says. "It embodies everything that's wrong with suburbia."

So I ask him to elaborate, and he's not at a loss for words. Max is a born-and-bred New Yorker. He's never at a loss for words.

"Don't you get it? The reason these idiots are floating around on their rafts is because they live in a place where Adult Swim is the only fifteen minutes per day they get to be an adult."

"Oh," I say.

"Adult swim is just a big Fuck You to their kids. Fuck you for making me move to the *sub*urbs! Fuck you for making me lose my identity! Fuck you for making me lose my edge!"

It's a typical Max rant, but I'd be lying if I said it doesn't somehow crystallize what's been at stake for me all summer.

I'd also be lying if I said I wasn't at Costco earlier that morning looking at the stainless steel gas barbecue grills they just got in for Labor Day.

If you're happy, your kids will be happy

What Max says about picking a place to raise your family.

If your kids are happy, you'll be happy

What I'd begun suspecting was closer to the truth.

If your wife is happy, you'll be happy

What my father says about picking a place to raise your family.

Oh really? Maybe he should have thought of that before our divorce

What my mother says when I tell her what my father says.

Adult Swim: could be worse

Following my inaugural fifteen-minute float, I am moved to contribute the only suggestion I've ever made to a suggestion box: piña coladas.

Another family is living in our house

It's a week before Labor Day. I pack up my minivan and drive back to Brooklyn so I can drop off some stuff before we move home. There's no place to park. There's a tiny smart car in front of our town house. It has Illinois plates, which means it belongs to our renters, which means I can double-park them in for a few minutes without worrying that they'll scrape my door with a key like our disturbed neighbor Sam did last year.

I liked Jake and Bonnie from the second I spotted their ad on craigslist. "Culture-Starved Family Seeks Summer in the City." They were teachers, so they got the summer off. They wanted their kids to experience the stimulation of the city. There was a symmetry to our situations. They were us, except opposite.

So I ring my own doorbell. Don't mind me, I tell Jake, I'll just be a few minutes. I'm holding my new MiniCraft Tabletop Hibachi Barbecue. Jake is multitasking. He's wearing my telephone headset and standing over my kitchen island. He's serving his two little kids bite-size pieces of the falafel platter he just had delivered from my favorite Middle Eastern place on Atlantic Avenue. His kids are crying. They're saying they didn't want falafel, they wanted *waffles*. And this is making it hard for Jake to hear whoever he's talking to on my headset—one of our babysitters, I'm guessing, because he keeps saying, "Seriously? Sixteen dollars an hour?" But I'm not here to eavesdrop. I'm here to unload my minivan. So I go back out and return with a couple of neon-green, Styrofoam swimming noodles. They're six feet long. They won't fit in the closet. It seems that Jake has his wife on my headset now. It seems that his wife might be late to the play tonight because the F train is only running on the A line and she can't find a cab. So Jake says he'll just pick her up in their car, their teeny-tiny little car, except he's worried they won't find a parking space when they get back to Brooklyn later that night. And now I can't help it. I have to interrupt. Alternate-side-of-the-street parking rules are in effect Tuesdays and Thursdays, I tell Jake, but the thing no one seems to realize is that night regulations allow you to park on *both* sides of the street from 7 p.m. to 8 a.m. except during declared snow emergencies, so as long as he wakes up early enough to move the car tomorrow morning, he should be fine. Except I'm not sure he hears me. His kids are really crying about that falafel platter. And thumping, Richter-scale bass vibrations have begun wafting in from a car stereo outside. So I go over to close the windows, and the thing I notice about them is this. The bars.

For the past eight weeks, we've lived in a house that didn't have iron security bars welded in front of the windows. I didn't even notice the bars when we first moved to Brooklyn. But over the years, they began lending a certain penal-colony aesthetic to the kitchen decor. One summer, Megan planted morning glory vines to wind around on the bars. It looked better than the bars, but a few months later, you couldn't see anything out the window. Except dead morning glory vines. And the ripped-up lottery tickets that get stuck in them on windy days.

Looking out my kitchen window now, there is one thing I can see perfectly clearly. A familiar neon-orange envelope has been placed beneath the windshield of my minivan.

Double parking. $250. I have been home fifteen minutes.

Dan Gets a Minivan

Acknowledgments

To paraphrase from *The Electric Kool-Aid Acid Test*, you're either on the minivan or off the minivan. Thanks to Jennifer Rudolph Walsh, my agent at WME, for being the first one on; and to Brant Rumble, my editor at Scribner, for steering us all to safety.

I'd also like to express my gratitude to the following rock stars:

Claudia Ballard, Christopher Barth, Brian Belfiglio, Amy Berkower, Abby Bluestone, Christine Bombard, Rex Bonomelli, Stephanie Booth, Anne Cherry, Erin Conroy, Esther Crain, Marlyn Dantes, Anna deVries, Mike Endelman, Whitney Frick, Doug Gochman, Judy Goldberg, Aimee Good, Alicia Gordon, Nan Graham, Frank Graziano Jr., Jake Guralnick, Erich Hobbing, Noelle Howey, Lyric Johnson, Ernie Karpelis, Shauna Keating, Stasia Kehoe, Gretchen Koss, Paul LaRocco, Lauren Lavelle, Adam Lichtenstein, Roz Lippel, Kevin MacRae, Jay Mandel, Scott Manning, Josh Margolis, Susan Moldow, Dana Points, Jonathan Putnam, Paul Raushenbush, Margaret Riley, Elisa Rivlin, Heather Rizzo, Elizabeth Sullivan, Keith Summa, Maura Tierney, Megan Tingley, Kristin van Ogtrop, Meg Walker, Kara Watson, Nina Willdorf, Laura Wise, Dan Zanes, and my fellow Zevins—Allyson, Barry, Bebe, Emma, Linda, Richard, Ron, and, especially, Josephine and Leo.

About the Author

Dan Zevin has been a comic correspondent for National Public Radio's WBUR, the humor columnist for *Boston* magazine and *The Boston Phoenix*, and a contributor to national publications including *Rolling Stone, Maxim, Details*, and *Parenting*. A Thurber Prize for American Humor finalist for *The Day I Turned Uncool: Confessions of a Reluctant Grown-up*, he is also the author of *Entry-Level Life* and *The Nearly-Wed Handbook*. Dan lives with his wife and their two children in the suburbs of New York City. He is an active member of his local Costco. For more information, visit www.danzevin.com.